The Decision-Makers

The Decision-Makers

*How to Improve the Quality of Decision-Making
in the Churches*

Lyle E. Schaller

ABINGDON PRESS
Nashville and New York

THE DECISION-MAKERS

Library of Congress Cataloging in Publication Data

SCHALLER, LYLE E. The decision-makers. Includes
bibliographical references. 1. Church management. 2.
Decision-making. I. Title.
BV652.S29   254   73-16411

ISBN 0-687-10402-5

Portions of this book are based on material which first appeared in two periodicals. Grateful acknowledgment is made
to the following publications:

The Clergy Journal, for "Should the Churches Subsidize the
Producers or the Consumers of Services?" (February, 1973).
Copyright 1972 by Church Management, Inc. Reprinted by
permission.

The Christian Advocate, for "Some Issues in Interchurch
Cooperation" (May 24, 1973). Copyright 1973 by The United
Methodist Publishing House. Reprinted by permission.

MANUFACTURED BY THE PARTHENON PRESS AT
NASHVILLE, TENNESSEE, UNITED STATES OF AMERICA

To
Edward P. Blair

Contents

Introduction

This book is an attempt to describe, analyze, and interpret the decision-making processes in the churches today. It also represents one part of a long-term effort to suggest means of improving the quality of decision-making in the churches.

It is based on the assumption that there is validity in the old saying "The beginning of wisdom is the understanding of reality." It is based on strong agreement with the contention of Daniel R. Grant, president of Ouachita Baptist University, that the politics of running government are no "dirtier" than decision-making in the churches. A longtime professor of political science at Vanderbilt University, Dr. Grant warned a seminar sponsored by the Christian Life Commission of the Southern Baptist Convention that those who believe religion and politics do not mix have a "counterfeit religion."

The focus in this book is largely on the process (the "how") of decision-making in the churches, rather than on the structure (the "who"), but of course it has not been possible to ignore structural considerations completely. If there is a theme or a central bias, it is that the institutional expression of the universal church can be understood only if it is perceived as both a religious organization and a voluntary association. When the decision-making processes are examined, the characteristics of the voluntary association, in which every member has the right of withdrawal, are as numerous and as influential as the other characteristics one would expect to find in an organized community of committed persons who accept Jesus Christ as Lord and Savior and turn to the Bible for their articles of faith.

Before moving on to offer the reader a "road map" describing the route followed in this volume, it is only fair to say a word about the baggage carried by the driver who chose the route and who will describe the scenery.

Like every other book about the life and ministry of the Christian church, this one rests on a long list of assumptions about the nature of contemporary reality. It may be helpful to identify a dozen which particularly influenced the author in the selection of material and in the interpretation of data.

The first, and also the most important, is that God is at work in the world today. Therefore the most significant way in which man can improve the quality of decision-making is by allowing the power of the Holy Spirit to be at work in it, in both the structures and the processes. This is easier to write than it is to accomplish, since on many occasions equally dedicated and committed Christians will differ on the best method of insuring that the power of the Holy Spirit can guide the decision-making process.

This leads to the second assumption: an acceptance of the Christian paradox that man is both good and bad. (See pages 177-79 for an elaboration of the impact of this assumption.) The Holy Spirit can be seen at work identifying the sinfulness of man as he rejects the Good News, and also convincing man of God's righteousness.

The third assumption is that God calls man to live and die in this world rather than to reject the world. Those who believe God is at work in the world he created cannot reject that world and remain faithful to God.

The fourth assumption is also the reason for including this list of the author's assumptions. Frequently the most influential force that a person brings to the decision-making process is the frame of reference that he uses to analyze the issues, to suggest solutions to problems, and to choose among alternative courses of action. The repeated references to this subject that are scattered throughout the book, and concentrated in chapters 2 and 8, reflect the importance attached to this subject. These twelve assumptions reflect one part of the author's frame of reference.

The fifth assumption has been stated earlier. The decision-making processes in the churches can be understood only if the various institutional expressions of the universal church are perceived as both religious organizations and voluntary associations. This means that the decision-making processes of the churches will always be influenced by what is happening in the other institutionalized segments of contemporary society, which is one excuse for including the last chapter of the book. It also means that there is always a tension between the limits of authority (permission) granted to a leader in a voluntary association by the members, who retain the right of withdrawal if they disagree with the decisions or actions of the leader, and the call to faithfulness and obedience that restricts the freedom of the person who is a member of a called-out community of the followers of Jesus Christ.

The sixth assumption has several facets and is a recurring theme of this volume. This is the assumption that it is rarely possible to "solve" problems. Frequently decision-making means trading one set of problems for a different set of problems. Usually this involves choosing from a comparatively long list of alternatives in making this "trade," a list that is often longer than many leaders realize. Rarely, however, is it possible for anyone to predict with certainty which set of problems from that list will turn out, in the light of a subsequent evaluation, to have been the best set. The only certainty is that the future is filled with a degree of uncertainty that would terrify, and perhaps immobilize, many decision-makers if they could foresee it accurately. This basic uncertainty about which alternative will turn out to be the best choice from a future perspective suggests that two useful criteria in choosing from among several alternatives are contained in these two questions: (1) Which alternative will *probably* keep the optimum number of choices open for the leaders of five or ten or twenty years hence? (2) Which alternative course of action will involve in the selection process the largest number of people who will have to live with the consequences of that decision and with a new set of problems?

The seventh assumption is that in the real world there is a

difference between programs of routine performance, in which certain actions are repeated, and strategies for planned change. This means that the ideas of scientific management, which trace back to Frederick Winslow Taylor and were described as "planning" by leading figures in the planning profession twenty-five years ago, do have relevance for improving the performance of an organization. The legacies of Taylor, which carry such contemporary labels as "operations research" and "systems analysis" can be utilized when the decision-making process is primarily concerned with improving the performance of an organization. The contemporary definitions of planning, however, are concerned with encouraging planned change and the maintenance of the necessary degree of organizational stability during this process of change. Most of the decision-making in the churches today is concerned with performance and not with strategies for change.

The eighth assumption, which undergirds much that is in this volume, is the conclusion that in most organizations, including all ecclesiastical organizations with more than thirty or forty members, the leaders do not constitute a representative cross section of the membership. The larger the membership, the greater the gap between the views and values of the leaders and those of the constituency.

The ninth assumption is closely related to the second and the eighth. The Christian doctrine of original sin helps explain the remarkably high degree of certainty many people feel about the correctness of their conclusions when they are making decisions for others. Among those most vulnerable to what can be described as "the First Commandment Problem" are preachers, presidents, politicians, planners, parents, publishers, authors, bishops, church leaders, and the decision-makers in any organization.

The tenth assumption is descriptive of the attempt to provide an overall frame of reference or context for this entire volume. This is the assumption that it is helpful if discussions of specific questions or detailed issues can be carried on within the context of a larger generalization, which may offer guidance on general policy considerations. Hopefully the contents of this volume are arranged so as to help the reader look at each issue from a larger and more inclusive frame of reference.

The eleventh assumption in this list is perhaps the most complex and certainly the most speculative! Frequently the decision-making process operates on three levels simultaneously. Some persons are operating on a descriptive level, trying to explain or to understand "how" it is. Usually it is possible (although this does not suggest that it is inevitable) to function on this level with a relatively high degree of certainty that what is said reflects reality accurately. The treasurer may state that there was a balance of $120 in the checking account as of this morning. That is how it is.

The next level concerns "why" it is that way. This moves the discussion to a more speculative level. At this level there is a sharp drop in the degree of confidence that what is said reflects present reality. Why is there a balance of $120 in the checking account?

The third level is the most speculative of all. This is the level at which the discussion moves to values. Is it "good" that there is a balance of $120 in the checking account? Or is it bad that the balance is $120?

It is assumed that the decision-making process can be improved if all the participants are functioning on the same level at any one point in the discussion.

It is also assumed that as the reader responds to the contents of this volume he or she will raise the question " Is my response on the level of how it is, or on the level of why it is that way, or on the level of values?" Hopefully there will be few occasions when the reader will find it necessary to disagree on the first level, with the descriptive statements or how it is. Inevitably there will be many occasions when the reader will disagree on the second level, about why it is that way. Many of the disagreements will be on the third level, on values. The reader's disagreements will probably be most creative and productive when they are concentrated on the top two levels.

The twelfth and final assumption is that if each participant in the decision-making process is consciously aware of the assumptions and the frame of reference that he or she carries into the process, this will improve the quality of decision-making in the churches.

As was pointed out earlier, the primary thrusts of this volume are intended to be descriptive and constructive. The first chapter is mainly descriptive, but a consistent effort has been made to offer an organized frame of reference for looking at how decisions are made. The perspective, or the frame of reference, of decision-makers is discussed more directly in the second chapter and, to a limited degree, again in chapter 8.

Three dimensions of the institutional and political nature of the decision-making processes of the churches are discussed in chapters 3, 4, and 5.

The greatest contributions of the Consultation on Church Union (COCU) have not been in the area of the organic union, where the efforts have been thwarted by a serious neglect of institutional considerations, but in encouraging a variety of forms of interchurch cooperation. Several lessons from the experiences of others in this arena of decision-making are summarized in chapter 6.

The decision-making processes in the churches are still tremendously influenced by an emphasis on the allocation of financial resources and by the quality and style of leadership. These two subjects are the focus for chapters 7 and 8.

The final two chapters are devoted more directly to suggestions for improving the quality of decision-making. Chapter 9 offers a frame of reference for examining the related subjects of accountability and evaluation, while the last chapter suggests several major points of increasing tension during the years ahead.

This book is dedicated to a teacher who has been an inspiration to many seminary students. I am only one of hundreds who owe so much to this warm, scholarly, and very human person, who served as a model, a witness, and a teacher of the Christian faith.

1 How Decisions Are Made

"Last fall we voted against going to two worship services on Sunday morning. Therefore that alternative is closed. About the only alternative left for us is to build," explained a trustee of the Oak Grove Church. He was describing the problem before that congregation, which was located in the second county out from a large metropolitan county. This ninety-year-old congregation had built a new brick meeting place on a four-acre site following a fire in 1961. Several years later the urban exodus began to produce a minor housing boom in the Oak Grove area. The congregation began to increase in size and to fill up the "new" building. On each of the last two Sundays a family had arrived a few minutes after the worship service began and walked all the way down to the front in search of a place, only to find even the front pews completely filled. The leader was arguing that, since a proposal to go to two services had been voted down earlier, he believed they should begin to plan an addition to the church building.

This incident illustrates one of the most subtle, but important, dimensions of the decision-making process. How does an issue or question begin to receive the serious consideration necessary for a meaningful decision?

Getting on the Agenda

The reply to the point raised by the trustee of the Oak Grove Church was that the alternative of scheduling two worship services on Sunday morning was not closed. It was still open. Being a rational individual who sought to use a logical approach to decision-making, he was both puzzled and incredulous on hearing this comment.

"I'm afraid you don't understand," he said. "The vote against going to two services was about 19 to 8. That door is closed! "

In looking at this incident, three generalizations can be offered that help to explain how decisions are made in voluntary organizations.

First, most major action proposals that mean a departure from tradition are voted down at least once before being adopted. The long list of examples includes the following. The Methodist Church in 1964 disapproved the recommendation that the name of the new denomination that would emerge from the union of the Methodists with the Evangelical United Brethren be " The United Methodist Church." The Euclid Avenue Christian Church in Cleveland, Ohio, voted against relocation and in favor of remaining at the 100-year-old location and remodeling the building; shortly after the remodeling was completed the congregation voted to relocate. A Lutheran parish in San Francisco voted 62 to 60 against a proposal to rent their building out on Sunday evenings for use by a metropolitan congregation of homosexuals, but soon after this vote they began a ministry to members of the gay community. The board of trustees of a seminary voted down a proposal to unite with another nearby theological school, and a few months later voted overwhelmingly in favor of the merger. The list includes literally hundreds of congregations which voted against a building proposal, and several months or perhaps a few years later went ahead with a building program. There are hundreds of situations where one or both of the congregations involved voted against a plan of union that would merge the two churches, and some time later the two united to form one congregation. The list also includes many congregations which now have two worship services on Sunday morning, but earlier had voted down a similar proposal.

The second generalization illustrated here is that one of the most common ways for a proposal to be placed on the agenda of a church is for it first to be presented, considered, and rejected. Most proposals that receive this much attention must be considered live options that may surface again for further attention.

Frequently, the process of getting a proposal for change on

the agenda is more subtle. A Presbyterian church seeking a new minister to replace their pastor, who had accepted a call to another congregation, finally narrowed the list of fifty possibilities down to four. The pulpit committee went to hear their first choice preach, and impressed, invited him over for an interview. After he had talked further with the members of the committee, toured the community, and seen the church building, it was clear that he was very favorably impressed, and the committee felt confident he would accept; so they took him over to see the fifty-five-year-old manse. As he walked through the empty house he said to the committee members, "I am tremendously impressed with the challenge and the opportunities here. This is about as close to my dream church as I could imagine. One thing this trip has done for me, however, is to help me see that I have not completed the work before me at the church I am now serving, and I'm afraid this is not the appropriate time for me to leave there. If this were two years hence I might be free to give affirmative consideration to a call, but I guess I'm really not free to leave this year."

After going through almost exactly the same process with the second and third ministers on their list, each of whom turned down the call when he saw the manse, they invited the fourth minister to come for an interview. He too was very favorably impressed with the committee members, the community, and the church building. When continued discussions indicated that if he expressed any more interest he would probably receive a call, he asked, "Now suppose you were to extend a call to me, I accepted, and the Presbytery approved—where would I live?"

"Oh, we're in the process of buying a new manse," was the reply, "but we don't want to make a final decision until our next minister has had a chance to be involved in the selection process."

The third generalization illustrated by the incident described at the beginning of this chapter is the vast difference between an affirmative and a negative vote on a proposal for change.

A negative response to the first proposal for change is often not a final rejection of the idea, but actually only a part of the process of getting the proposal on the agenda for further consideration.

By contrast, not only does an affirmative vote tend to have a far greater degree of finality, but some types of affirmative decisions are also the most effective means of eliminating alternative courses of action from the list of available options. A negative vote on a proposal for change is not necessarily final, but a favorable vote often does eliminate alternatives that were never directly voted down.

Thus in the Oak Church the vote against a proposal to change to two worship services on Sunday morning need not be considered a final decision. By contrast not only would an affirmative vote on enlarging the worship facilities probably lead to implementation of that alternative, but such a building program would probably also eliminate any serious consideration of the two-service alternative for many years. Frequently the critical vote against a proposed course of action is not the vote that rejects that proposal, but a subsequent vote to implement a course of action that by its nature reduces the options. Thus a vote at Oak Grove to change to two worship services on Sunday morning does not eliminate the possiblity of a shift to two worship services on Sunday morning.

Consensus or Majority?

A person can be elected to the office of President of the United States by 50 percent plus one of the votes in the electoral college. In many states 51 percent of the voters can approve an increase in the tax rate and that decision is binding on all taxpayers.

In voluntary associations, however, where the right of withdrawal is less restricted, a simple majority is often not enough to make a decision that will be binding on all parties. For example, the General Conference of the Evangelical Association (the same Evangelical church that merged with the Church of the United Brethren in Christ in 1946) voted by a one-vote margin to unite with the Methodist Episcopal Church. But the presiding bishop ruled that a one-vote majority was insufficient to carry a motion for such a radical change, and declared the motion lost. In terms of parliamentary procedure that presiding bishop was in error, since the rules of the conference required only a simple majority vote to adopt a motion. But in terms of how a voluntary association makes and implements a decision, he was absolutely correct. Any decision for a major change in a voluntary association normally requires the support of a consensus, not simply 50 percent plus one, if it is to be implemented effectively and without disruptive consequences.

When this generalization is ignored the consequences may be both surprising and disruptive. Two pastors who had not seen each other for several years were talking, and the first asked, "Why did you leave St. Paul's after only two years?" The second replied, "While serving as president of the church council I ruled that a motion in favor of a $285,000 building program was carried when a count of the ballots revealed 16 for the motion and 15 opposed. When the building fund drive produced $141,000 in pledges, I decided it might be best for me to seek a call to another parish."

Influencing Decisions

A Swedish Lutheran Church saw that it was outgrowing its small white frame building and needed more space. As the leaders discussed the problem a dozen potential new locations were considered. None of them could gain the support of more than two or three of the men on the committee. Two months later two of the older members of the parish came to a meeting of the committee and said, "We have an option to purchase the site at the corner of Lake Road and Hillside. If this committee will recommend that site to the congregational meeting as the place to relocate, we'll buy it and give the land to the church. But remember, our option is only for thirty days, so we have to have an answer by the tenth of next month." On the sixth of the month the congregation voted 137 to 17 in favor of accepting a gift of that property as the relocation site.

"This is not an action motion," argued a member of Emmanuel Church as a motion to continue investigation of the possibility of sponsoring a housing-for-the-elderly project was being debated at the annual congregational meeting. "You will have a chance later to decide whether we should actually sponsor a housing project. All this motion does is permit the committee to continue its investigations, plans, and negotiations. They cannot go ahead without a clear affirmative congregational vote on a specific proposal. The critical vote on whether we actually go ahead with a housing-for-the-elderly project will come later. At that time you will have a chance to cast a decisive yes or no vote. All this motion does is to authorize the committee to continue its feasibility and planning studies."

Several months later those present at a specially called congregational meeting were told, "When you authorized the planning and feasibility studies you gave a green light to this project if the studies indicated it was a feasible project. A total of $60,000 has been spent on these studies. If you vote against this motion, that means $60,000 down the drain. If you vote for the motion, it means the $60,000 can be credited toward Emmanuel's equity in this project. If you didn't want us to go ahead with the project, you should have voted against the motion to continue these studies back at our annual meeting in January."

In both of these illustrations the formal vote was actually a matter of bringing people together to approve, on the basis of financial commitments already made rather than on the merits of the proposal itself, a decision that had already been made by a small group of people.

"One of Us"

Among the considerations that influence how decisions are made, one of the most significant factors in the churches, as well as all across society, is the "we-they" division. This can be illustrated by the exceptionally influential role of Italians in the Vatican, or by the ready acceptance by a rural congregation of a denominational executive who was reared on a farm, or by the attitudes of the people from the smaller denomination for years after the merger of a small denomination with a much larger one.

"Is he one of us?" This unspoken question is frequently asked about strangers, visiting church bureaucrats, prospective new pastors for a congregation, and proponents of a change from the status quo. Thus, in talking with a pastor in The Lutheran Church–Missouri Synod, it is often helpful to know whether he graduated from Concordia Seminary in St. Louis or Concordia Seminary in Springfield, Illinois. If a denominational staff person is to visit a parish of The American Lutheran Church in central Illinois, it will make a tremendous difference with certain congregations if the person sent is an East Friedlander. The East Friedlanders are descended from residents of the northwestern part of Germany, and they easily identify with one another. Congregations of East Friedlanders usually have remarkable records of church attendance, giving, and outreach. They are also exceptionally loyal, and another East Friedlander can evoke that loyalty.

The importance of this attitude has been heightened by the denominational unions of recent years. Thus a United Presbyterian minister may be asked whether he came from the Presbyterian Church in the U.S.A. or from the United Presbyterian Church of North America. In considering prospective ministers some congregations of the United Church of Christ are still concerned about whether a candidate comes from the Evangelical and Reformed or the Congregational Christian side of that merger. In a few places, especially in Pennsylvania, a further distinction is made between Reformed and Evangelical, although the merger of those two denominations occurred in 1934.

Likewise some decide whether the person is "one of us" on

the basis of where he went to school. In the 1940s and the 1950s the "in" groups in some midwestern conferences of The Methodist Church were drawn largely from the graduates of the Boston University School of Theology. There is still an advantage in many parts of the South for the minister of the Presbyterian Church in the U.S. who graduated from Davidson College in North Carolina and Union Theological Seminary in Virginia. Asking where a minister went to seminary is often used as a means of identifying allies for an expected legislative battle at the annual denominational meeting as well as for screening candidates for a vacant pulpit. While not an especially reliable method, the use of this question is an interesting example of the use of code words in decision-making.

The Impact of Tradition

Closely related to the "Is he one of us?" question is the impact of tradition and custom on the structures and the decision-making processes in the churches.

What is the most influential force on the allocation of income in next year's budget in the church? The obvious answer, the amount of the anticipated income, is usually the *second* most important factor. In most ecclesiastical agencies last year's budget is the most influential single force in determining the allocations in next year's budget.

Why does St. John's Church, with a membership of 500, an average attendance at Sunday morning worship of 220, and total receipts of $70,000, have two ministers on the staff, while St. Paul's Church, with 600 members, an average attendance of 300, and congregational receipts of $90,000, has only one minister on the staff? Probably one reason is that for at least fifteen years St. John's has had two ministers, and St. Paul's has never had more than one.

Why are there two Episcopal churches in downtown Elmira, New York? Because one is "low church" and one is Anglo-Catholic? Though that is one reason, a more important factor is that there have been two for over a century as a result of a division among Episcopalians over slavery. Following the severe flood of 1972, which inflicted substantial damage on the extensive buildings of both congregations, some argued that the two should unite. Tradition won, however.

What is the most distinctive characteristic of the Wabash Association of the Illinois Conference of the United Church of Christ? That it covers a clearly defined geographical area as do the other associations of the conference? No. The distinctive characteristic of the Wabash Association is that it is composed entirely of congregations that were in the Christian Church, which in 1931 united with the Congregational Church to form the General Council of the Congregational Christian Churches, which in 1957 united with the Evangelical and Reformed Church to form the United Church of Christ. Tradition, however, maintains a small association of what were formerly Christian Churches.

Why are so many graduates of Augustana Theological Seminary serving as pastors in the Pacific Southwest Synod of the Lutheran Church in America? One reason may be that, following the consolidation in 1962 of the Augustana Evangelical Lutheran Church and three other denominations into the Lutheran Church in America, California became a stronghold of the Augustana branch of the Lutheran family.

Why is there one nongeographical district in The Lutheran Church–Missouri Synod, when all the rest of the synod is organized into geographical districts? Because of race, nationality, or color, as has been the basis for organizing nongeographical administrative units in other denominations? No; the history of this English District traces back over a century to when a number of Lutheran pastors, dissatisfied with the General Council of the Lutheran Church in Tennessee and West Virginia, sought fellowship with the conservative Lutheran Church–Missouri Synod through its president, Dr. C. F. W. Walther. Upon Walther's urging they organized the English Conference. A quarter of a century later, when it was discovered that God is at least bilingual, the German Missouri

Synod accepted the much smaller "English Missouri Synod" as a separate, nongeographical district. So they have continued as a separate, nongeographical district, and as one of the more progressive groups in the synod.

The location of the headquarters for a regional judicatory recently became a major issue as a result of a merger of two denominations and the subsequent restructuring of the administrative apparatus. One group wanted to move the headquarters to a larger city in the north central part of the state. Another group wanted to move it to the largest city in the judicatory in the northwest part of the state. Each group presented a very persuasive case in favor of its chosen location. Both lost. Why? One reason was that neither group presented any direct arguments against continuing the headquarters at the old location, and so the committee recommended remaining at the traditional location. Thus the committee validated once again the basic law of traditionalism: If it is not necessary to change, it is necessary not to change.

Reducing the Power of Tradition

Tradition and custom do not always carry the day, however, when churches make decisions. There are a number of forces that, under the appropriate set of circumstances, can offset the impact of tradition. One of these is a perceived crisis.

The session of a Presbyterian church had an official, but unwritten, policy that Negroes would not be received into membership in that congregation. After the highly popular minister of two decades retired, a pulpit committee was selected and began interviewing candidates. After refusals from the three most promising candidates when each learned of this restriction, the pulpit committee delivered an ultimatum to the session: "Either change the policy on barring Negroes from membership or we won't be able to find a pastor." The session reluctantly reversed the policy.

A few years after the denominational merger of the Evangelical Church with the United Brethren in Christ the 200-member Bethel Evangelical United Brethren Church united with the First Evangelical United Brethren Church, which had just seen its building destroyed by fire. The new united congregation adopted the name First Evangelical United Brethren Church. Fifteen years later the merger with Methodists produced two congregations called First United Methodist Church with their buildings only a few blocks apart. Both agreed to change their names. The former Methodist congregation changed its name to Wesley United Methodist Church. The traditionalists in the former Evangelical United Brethren congregation urged that congregation to go back and pick up the name Bethel. There was almost unanimous support for this decision until someone pointed out that the acronym would be less than ideal. Ridicule can occasionally offset tradition.

The Southern Baptist Convention has had a long history of opposition to direct federal aid to religious organizations. This tradition traces back to the struggles of Separatists in seventeenth-century England. By the middle 1960s the convention had become deeply involved with this issue. On the one side were the pressures of principle and tradition. On the other side were the pressures of Southern Baptist schools and hospitals which needed a larger income to offset rising costs. In 1967 the Kentucky Baptist Convention released Kentucky Baptist College from control by the state convention to free it to secure federal aid. Financial pressures also may offset tradition.

A denominational committee planning for new churches was in the process of selecting sites for three new churches. Over the years the committee had developed a set of criteria for selection of church sites, including such considerations as size, shape, frontage, accessibility, visibility, and drainage. The committee was about to purchase a well-drained and improved four-acre site with 400 feet of frontage on a major street for $30,000, when a developer offered them a free three-acre site at the end of a block in a subdivision he was planning. Though the site was located on a thirty-foot residential street near the center of the development and a mile from even a secondary collector street, the committee concluded that in the interests of good stewardship it could not afford to reject the developer's offer. After paying for street, sidewalk, sewer, and water assessments on the three sides of the lot and installing a storm water drainage system, the church had invested $33,000 in the property. Even the mirage of relief from financial pressures may offset tradition.

For decades it has been a tradition in The Lutheran Church–Missouri Synod that a clergyman called to serve as the pastor of a congregation should receive a lifetime call. In 1972, however, the surplus of pastors which had already been felt by several other denominations began to catch up with the Missouri Synod. When in 1972 it appeared that the number of seminary graduates might begin to exceed the number of calls, it became possible for two-year calls to be extended to, and accepted by, graduates of the denomination's two seminaries. Even in a denomination where tradition is unusally influential, it is possible for an impending crisis to cause a revision of tradition.

The first Baptist congregation in Toledo, Ohio, to become an "open membership" church did so when three traditions collided. A merger with a Presbyterian congregation in 1929 provided that the building owned by the Presbyterian church would be the meeting place of the new united congregation. A number of Presbyterians did not want to abandon their tradition of baptism by sprinkling, nor did they want to leave their traditional meeting place. As a result the Baptist church became an open-membership congregation which received into full membership persons who had not been immersed.

The Location of Decision-Making

Beginning in late 1972 the federal government began returning to the states substantial sums of money in undesignated block grants known as "revenue sharing." A complex formula required that some of these monies be passed on to counties and municipalities. The funds for revenue sharing became available by a combination of (*a*) reducing federal expenditures for such programs as vocational rehabilitation, subsidized housing, the Office of Economic Opportunity, agricultural subsidies and (*b*) continuing a comparatively large deficit in the federal budget.

How were those funds used that were passed on to counties and municipalities? A large share of the total was used for wage and salary increases for employees of local governments, the purchase of fire trucks, repair of county roads, the construction of new municipal and county buildings, a reduction in the general property tax, and improvement of local sewage disposal systems. Only a tiny proportion of these funds was used by state and local governments for housing for low-middle- and low-income families, public assistance, education, or aid to the poor.

Revenue sharing stands out as a remarkably clear example of how the "location" of the decision-making point in the allocation of public funds significantly influences how those funds are allocated.

A parallel can be seen in the churches. The number of dollars available to the national board of home missions, the national social action agency, and the national board of Christian education of several denominations began to level off beginning in 1968 and 1969. The dollar income of the congregations that contributed these funds to the national agencies continued to increase, although not as rapidly as in the 1950–65 period. In a few denominations, including the United Church of Christ and the Episcopal Church, the actual income of some national agencies declined while the income of congregations continued to rise. There was a sharp increase in the amounts allocated by congregations and local judicatories for "outreach and missions" in most denominations.

While it would be either an exaggeration or a joke to describe this as an intentional program of revenue sharing by the national denominational agencies, the effect has been similar. If these funds can be viewed as monies which might have been expended by a national agency but in fact are being allocated by congregations and regional judicatories, two important changes can be identified as resulting from the change in the location of these decisions. First, persons in the congregational and regional places of decision-making now feel a much stronger sense of "ownership" of the programs for which the funds are used, and therefore they are much more willing to defend the allocation of church funds for these causes. Second, the nature of the programs receiving church funding has changed. Less money is going into social action programs such as race relations, civil rights, help for American Indians, support for open housing legislation, and anti-poverty efforts. But far more money is going from the churches into day care centers, nursery schools, counseling for the mentally ill, direct help for the elderly, ministries to alienated youth in upper-middle-income suburbs, adult education, and combating drug addiction.

In a very predictable manner the swing toward the decentralization of power that has been a trend in several main-line Protestant denominations since 1968 has not only changed the place of decision-making in the allocation of church funds, but has also drastically altered the order of the priorities. When the swing back toward centralization begins to accelerate, it too will change both the place of decision-making and the order of priorities in the allocation of the outreach money of the churches. How decisions are made is influenced by where they are made!

Decisions or Choices?

"What is the ideal Sunday morning schedule for a suburban church today?"

"Is it better to have all the staff members in the regional judicatory working out of one office and living in the same city, or is it better to deploy the staff so they live in various sections of the state and work out of their homes?"

"What is the best length of time for a minister to serve the same congregation? Five years? Six years? Eight years? Ten years? Fifteen years? Twenty years?"

These three questions illustrate a basic fact of decision-making today. Rarely do people have the opportunity to make a decision which will result in putting all the positive factors on one side of the equation and all the negative factors on the other. Most decisions are actually the process of choosing among several alternatives, each one of which has attractive features and also unattractive characteristics. In each of these three questions, as well as in most other issues, the choice is not between a "right" answer and a "wrong" answer. In the real world, making a choice between two alternatives is choosing one set of problems in preference to another set of problems. The congregation that changes from one worship service to two on Sunday morning, or vice versa, does not "solve" all its problems by that decision. It merely trades one set of problems for a different set of problems. When the decision-making process is examined in this context such words as *trade-off* and *compromise* become more meaningful.

This frame of reference can be used in analyzing the problem-solving and decision-making processes in any organization. Which set of problems would you prefer to live with in terms of your capabilities and resources? Will this change mean "trading up" for a more desirable set of problems or "trading down" for a less attractive set of problems?

In looking at these questions it is helpful to list the criteria which can be used in selecting the set of problems that will accompany a final decision.

The question of the Sunday morning schedule is an example of this. The criteria for deciding on the schedule for Sunday morning might include these: Which schedule will provide the most attractive hour(s) for corporate worship? Which will provide the best opportunities for adult Christian education experiences? Which will strengthen the Sunday School? Which will enable the church school teachers to attend worship regularly? Which will be most acceptable to the choir(s)? Which will provide for the most meaningful use of the pastor's time? Which will strengthen meaningful fellowship opportunities? Which will be most attractive to persons who are not members, but whom we are trying to reach on Sunday morning? Which will be the least disruptive change from the present schedule? Which will be most conducive to attainment of the basic goals of the church? Which provides the optimum range of meaningful choices for people? Which choices are severely limited by the building facilities? Which will create the fewest traffic problems?

A similar approach can be used in deciding whether synod or conference should be centralized or geographically decentralized, and in deciding when a pastor should move. Building a list of criteria helps identify the advantages and the problems that are a part of each alternative.

The Four Basic Decision Situations

Sometimes it helps to look at the context of decision-making. Specialists in operations research have suggested that there are four basic decision situations.[1] These can be illustrated by decisions you might have to make if you were a pastor.

1. Decision-Making Under Certainty

What topic will you preach on next Sunday? It is certain that you are expected to lead the morning worship service next Sunday, and the members of the congregation assume you will preach a sermon. The certainty is that (barring an unforeseen set of circumstances) you will deliver a sermon. The uncertainty (the area of decision-making) is the text and the content.

2. Decision-Making Under Risk

You are very busy this week, and to the best of your knowledge no one from your parish is in the hospital; so you decide not to stop by the hospital on Tuesday and Friday as you usually do.

There is a risk that one of your members may be in the hospital or may go in and no one will notify you because they will assume that you will be stopping in on Tuesday and Friday. There is a risk that you may fail to make what could have been a very meaningful call.

3. Decision-Making Under Conflict

The high school youth group in your church wants to have a dance every Saturday night in the fellowship hall. As you talk with different members about this, two of your leading families warn that the day a dance is held in the church will be the day they leave it. Your best friend in the congregation advises that pushing the proposal could split the congregation. Your son says that if you fail to support the young people they will write you off completely as a part of the anti-youth Establishment.

4. Decision-Making Under Uncertainty

You have been asked to leave the congregation where you have been the pastor for five years to serve as the pastor for a yet-to-be-organized nongeographical parish that will be drawn from nineteen- to twenty-five-year-olds working in the Loop in Chicago. This is your denomination's first attempt anywhere in the nation to develop a new, autonomous, self-governing, and self-supporting congregation of this type.

The basic value of the situational frame of reference in examing the decision-making process is that it helps determine the type of approach that will probably be followed in the effort to reach a decision.

In the first situation, decision-making under certainty, one uncontrollable variable is known. In the second category an additional variable is added, but it can be quantified. In the third situation the variables are more complex, and this is where the use of "games" or simulation exercises begins to be useful in testing possible strategies. The fourth situation, decision-making under uncertainty, is where judgment is at a premium.

Typically an individual or an organization will make decisions unilaterally in the first two situations (which cover well over 98 percent of all decisions), but with some hesitation in the case of decisions made under risk. In the third type of situation, decision-making under conflict, the tendency in ecclesiastical organizations is to search for a compromise that will dissolve or avoid the conflict. In general, the higher up in the hierarchy of an organization that a decision is being made, the more likely it is that the decision-making will be either under conflict or under uncertainty.[2]

When faced with the fourth situation, decision-making under uncertainty, religious organizations tend either (a) to postpone making a decision or (b) to call in outsiders to advise them (and thus to share the blame if the chosen course of action turns out to be disappointing). This pattern is illustrated by the congregation in a changing neighborhood, by the seminary that suddenly realizes its future existence is highly uncertain, by the executive in the regional judicatory that will be merging with another regional judicatory as a result of a forthcoming denominational merger, and by the board of a denominational camp that sees a diminishing number of campers using the facility each summer. Frequently the delay in making a decision eliminates most of the options that were open earlier when the degree of uncertainty was greatest. Eventually all the alternative courses of action except one or two have been eliminated by the passage of time. This simplifies the task of the decision-maker, although it often produces decisions of inferior quality.

Types of Decisions

The eminent sociologist Talcott Parsons has described three types of decisions in contemporary organizations.[3] The first of these is the *policy* decision. The generalized decision to establish an organization or to abolish an existing agency would be a policy decision. The second type is the *allocative* decision, in which the resources of an organization are allocated in an effort to attain certain goals. This may be the assignment of responsibilities among personnel, or the allocation of financial resources to a specific program. *Integrative* decisions, intended to facilitate the operation of the organization, constitute the third variety.

The distinction between these three types of decisions is illustrated by the experience of the Main Street Baptist Church. This 600-member, seventy-five-year-old congregation had been meeting at the same location since the day construction of its first building was completed. In 1968 the leaders began to become aware of the gradual dispersal of the congregation. A survey in 1959 had revealed that three-fifths of the members lived within a mile of the church. By 1967 the proportion had dropped to one-third. Following a series of detailed studies a special planning committee decided to recommend that the church relocate to a suburban community. If adopted this would be a *policy* decision. A congregational meeting was called for February 6, 1969, to receive and act on this recommendation. At noon on that day it began to snow, and by early evening the streets were virtually impassable. Despite the bad weather twenty-six members showed up for the meeting, and it was obvious from the conversation that most of them favored relocation.

When the meeting was finally called to order the chairman said, "Friends, as you know, the constitution of our church states that 20 members constitute a quorum for the purpose of doing business at a congregational meeting. Like most of you I favor relocation, and I am anxious to get this settled and move on to selecting a site for a new church. However, I don't believe it is fair to the members who could not get here tonight, to decide such an important question with so few present. I had hoped we would have 150 or more members here for this discussion. Therefore I am suggesting we adjourn and reschedule the meeting for two weeks from tonight."

37

After a brief discussion it was agreed to adjourn without a vote on the question of relocation. This was an *integrative* decision. Everyone present realized that the process of relocation would test the loyalty of many members. If the decision to relocate was made at a meeting attended by less than 5 percent of the members this would increase the tensions in an already divided congregation. Organizational peace and harmony made it advisable to postpone the decision.

Later, after a favorable vote on relocation, the congregation voted to place the proceeds from the sale of the Main Street property in the newly created building fund and elected a building committee which consisted of seven of the ablest members of the church. This was an *allocative* decision in which personnel and resources were assigned as part of the goal attainment (relocation) process.

This distinction between the three basic types of organizational decisions can be very helpful in the effort to understand how and why decisions are made. A denomination planning a large national convocation assigns quotas to the different regional judicatories. An Eastern judicatory fills its quota and asks for more places but is refused, despite the fact that it is clear that the Southwestern area will probably not use its quota. A member of the convocation is puzzled and asks, "If there are people in the East who want to come, why don't we accept their applications? Our goal is to get a big turnout, isn't it?" The chairman replies, "It is important that we have a large crowd, but it is even more important that we have a representative number from each part of the country so that no part of our church feels left out." The committee supports the chairman and makes an *integrative* decision, although it may appear at first to be an *allocative* decision.

Usually the *policy* decisions are the most important in any organization, and people who like to be at the power center often seek membership on the policy committees. In American Protestantism, however, unlike most large private corporations and many public agencies, there is seldom a clear demarcation between the place where policies are decided and the one where allocative decisions are made. Frequently the policy emerges out of the allocative decisions.

For example, one rarely finds an active policy committee in a Protestant congregation. Policy decisions are usually made by the same people who make the allocative decisions. There is nothing wrong with this except that too often policy decisions are derived from the allocative decisions and thus are of less value. The persons who count the trees sometimes cannot see the forest.

The same situation frequently prevails on the denominational level, where the policy decisions are really made by the committee in charge of the allocation of the financial resources. The results are often most visible at the annual meeting of the denomination, where the assembled delegates think of themselves as the policy-makers. They have come together to review last year's work, to listen to reports and proposals, and to make the basic policy decisions which will guide next year's efforts at building the Kingdom. Frequently something else appears to happen. The real division of power is uncovered only when the delegates attempt to initiate policy rather than simply rubber-stamp decisions that are an integral part of the reports they receive from the boards and committees.

Suppose Roy Jenkins, a lay delegate from the church at Eagle Pass, stands up and is recognized by the chair. "I have sat here for two days and listened to all of the reports. I have studied all of the statistics that have been hurled at us. It seems to me we are spending a lot of money, but we aren't doing a thing for one group in our church who need our help. I am referring to our older church members who have a limited income and find it hard to get a decent place to live in their old age. I move that we delegates instruct the people in charge of getting up the programs and spending our mission gifts that first priority be given to building and operating a home for the elderly." The motion receives an immediate second and obviously has overwhelming support from the delegates. After all, this is a very sympathetic group. Like most denominational meetings, this one is held during the daytime in the middle of the week, and as a result over two-thirds of the lay delegates are past or near retirement age. Besides, who could vote against such an obviously meritorious proposal?

This is clearly a generalized policy decision. In response to a question, Mr. Jenkins makes it clear that he wants to leave the details of location, site, size, cost, financing, and operation to a special committee. This is simply a decision to assign priorities.

What happens when the delegates try to initiate policy in a situation such as this?

One possibility would be for no one to take any of the actions necessary for implemention of this motion by the delegates. If a special committee is not appointed, and if Mr. Jenkins is not a delegate to next year's annual meeting, nothing will happen.

Another possibility would be for a member of the finance committee to ask for the floor after the motion is seconded. "As a member of your finance committee," he begins, "I feel the responsibility to raise this question. Where is the money coming from to build the home? Earlier today you adopted a budget for the coming year which allocates every dollar we expect to receive from the churches. Does this motion overrule that action? Does this "first priority" clause mean that the new home will get first call on all receipts and that the other causes will divide what is left over? Certainly this subject is one dear to the hearts of us all. I'll be retiring after four more years and I would dearly love to have a place like this where my wife and I could go and spend the rest of our years. This could be a very expensive program, however, and could seriously cripple the rest of our programs. Therefore I would like to offer a substitute motion that this matter be referred to the finance committee so methods of financing can be studied."

What this man is really saying is, "You delegates are attempting to make an important policy decision here on the floor of the meeting. You can't do that! You should know that all of the policy decisions involving money are made by our finance committee. If this is a proposal to make policy, let's get it into the finance committee, where it will receive the careful attention of a group of responsible policy-makers. We on the committee are not about to let our power to make policy be taken over by the delegates. If, during the next year, we feel enough pressure, you can rest assured that we'll find some money to get this started. We'll compromise rather than surrender our power, but we're not going to give up this easily!"

If one of the delegates recognizes the distinction between policy and allocative decisions, he may be able to persuade his colleagues that they do have the authority to make policy decisions and that here is a chance to exercise that authority. Thus a motion would be in order which instructed the finance committee to give first priority to the request from a special committee on a home for the elderly in preparing *next year's* proposed budget. This would probably be an acceptable motion. It might not result in the wisest expenditure of the Lord's money, but it would recognize the distinction between the policy-making authority of the annual meeting and the allocative authority of the finance committee.

Influences on the Process

Throughout all stages of the process and in all types of decisions there are pressures on the decision-makers which affect them and their decisions. These influences range from friendship ties to prejudices instilled in childhood, from a lust for power to an urge to avoid responsibility, from a nostalgic longing for "the good old days" to a desire for change, and from a perception of a crisis to a desire to do good. Several of these pressures were illustrated in the early sections of this chapter.

The Three Basic Power Centers

Earlier, reference was made to the location or place of the decision-making process, and it was pointed out, using revenue sharing as one illustration, that the place where the decision is made often greatly influences the content of that decision.

In most denominations in American Protestantism there are three major centers of power—the congregation, the regional judicatory of the denomination, and the national denominational agencies.[4] Within each of these there is not one single power structure, but rather a cluster of power centers, the influence of each varying with the issue, the circumstances, and the time. In the 1920s and the 1950s, for example, the Sunday School was a stronger power center in many congregations than it was in the late 1960s and early 1970s. The influence of the women's organization as a major power center has been declining in both denominations and congregations for the past quarter-century. In general the influence of the pastor has been declining in recent years with the emergence of a shared leadership style of pastoral role (see chapter 8).

When the three basic levels of power are examined, it appears that the power and influence of the congregation have been diminishing during this century as part of the general trend in society toward increased centralization. A more precise statement would be that while the total influence of the congregation is diminishing and the power of the regional and national judicatories is increasing, there are many exceptions to this (see chapters 5, 6, 7, and 8). In most denominations, starting in the middle or late 1960s, the power of the congregation began to increase slightly, the power of the regional judicatory continued to increase, and the influence of the national judicatories declined. This coincided with a basic movement toward decentralization all across American society. When the pendulum begins to swing back toward centralization, probably by the later 1970s, there will again be a shift in the relative influence of the three basic levels of power.

Steps in Decision-Making

In reviewing how decisions are made in the churches, it is possible to break the process down into a series of steps. The number of steps will depend on how much detail is desired. The simplest way to describe the process is as the interaction of fact and desire. The three basic steps in any decision-making process are (1) initiation, (2) approval, and (3) execution. A more detailed analysis describes a twelve-step process.[5]

1. Preliminary agreement on the question
2. Analysis of the facts
3. Listing of alternative courses of action
4. Review in the context of overall policy
5. A more detailed examination of the facts
6. Review of probable consequences of each alternative
7. Elimination of several alternatives
8. Analysis of all possible consequences of each of the remaining alternatives
9. Selection and recommendation of one or two alternative courses of action
10. Formal communication of that recommendation to members of the final decision-making group
11. A formal decision
12. Implementation

Whether the decision concerns the purchase of new robes for the choir, the selection of a site for relocation of the meeting place of the congregation, the future use of a denominational camp, or the complete restructuring of a denominational organization, all twelve steps are part of that process.

This chapter has suggested how decisions are made in the churches, and a few methods of analyzing the process. Before going on to examine specific subjects in more detail, it may be helpful to examine more carefully the importance of the frame of reference that each party brings to the decision-making process.

2 What Is Your Frame of Reference ?

A fact without a theory
Is like a ship without a sail,
Is like a boat without a rudder,
Is like a kite without a tail.
A fact without a figure
Is a tragic final act,
But one thing worse
In this universe
Is a theory without a fact.

George Schultz[1]

The systematic participant in any decision-making process has a specific example to illustrate every generalization—and also a generalization that provides the context for every specific comment, suggestion, or criticism.

Most clergymen are trained to be conscious of the importance of the first half of that statement. Every course in public speaking stresses the value of relevant illustrations. By the time he reaches his fortieth birthday the successful politician, the typical community leader, or the experienced preacher has accumulated such a large and varied collection of interesting stories, embarrassing events, humorous anecdotes, and fascinating vignettes that he can offer a specific illustration for any generalization.

Far less common, however, is the ability to put forward the theory, the policy or set of basic assumptions, or the generalization, that offers a meaningful and helpful context for evaluating facts and considering specific action proposals. One of the most effective ways of improving the quality of the decision-making process is to examine every question, problem, issue, or proposed course of action from within the context of a relevant generalization.

This applies not only to decision-makers, but also to every person seeking to understand reality. In his comparison of the work and contributions of Charles A. Beard and Carl Becker

44

as historians, Page Smith wrote, "The man with a system, however inadequate it may ultimately turn out to be, has a vast advantage over a systemless rival, however brilliant." [2]

The importance of having a system is illustrated by the efforts to plan for the future of a specific congregation. In one case, for example, seven members of a small rural church fifty miles from the center of a huge metropolitan area were meeting one Sunday afternoon to talk about the future of that ninety-member congregation. Each participant brought to the discussion a generalization about the type of church to which they belonged. One saw it as a former rural congregation in the process of becoming suburban; a couple contended that the transformation had already occurred; while the oldest man present still saw it as a congregation of farm families. Perhaps the greatest obstacle in this group's efforts to plan for the future was the insistence on discussing detailed specific questions without attempting to clarify each question by discussing the basic assumptions that each held to be the appropriate context for it.

While it usually facilitates the decision-making process if all participants have the same "system" or frame of reference, it is more important for each to be aware of and to understand the frame of reference of the other participants. Agreement is less significant than understanding.

This impact of differing perspectives and sets of assumptions on decision-making can be clarified by lifting up a few that stand out in any analysis of the decision-making processes in the churches.

The Real Lay-Clergy Gap

Perhaps the most important, and certainly the most common, example of how differences in the frame of reference influence the decision-making process can be seen in the "lay-clergy gap." The heart of this gap lies in the differences in perspectives.

45

In general terms, ministers tend to differ from the laity on several matters:

1. What are the most decisive criteria for measuring the "success" of the church? Pastors tend to emphasize size, outreach, missions, evangelism, the quality of people's spiritual life, and a sense of faithfulness. Lay persons tend to emphasize statistical growth or decline (which is a vastly different subject from size); the health, vigor, and size of the Sunday School; finances; and buildings.

2. What is the orientation in time? Pastors tend to be oriented toward today and tomorrow. Lay persons tend to display a stronger orientation toward yesterday and today. (One obvious explanation for this difference is that in most congregations the adults among the laity have been members of that congregation for a far longer period of time than the pastor has. Therefore they remember "yesterday" with greater clarity than he does. A second reason is that in the majority of congregations the age of the minister is below the median age of the lay leadership.)

3. What is the appropriate leadership style for the pastor? A larger proportion of ministers favor a shared leadership style than is the case with lay persons. Lay people tend to prefer the pastor to be *the leader*, whereas ministers tend to prefer that the pastor be seen as *one* of the leaders.

4. What were the outstanding events in this parish during the last year? When asked this question the laity tend to have a very short list and to think in terms of (a) what happened to them individually and (b) what happened to the parish in institutional terms. Pastors tend (naturally) to have a much longer list and to respond with (a) events that stood out from the regular rhythm of the parish, (b) effective ventures in outreach, evangelism, and missions, (c) areas of interchurch cooperation, and (d) relationships with the denomination.

5. What is the conceptual framework for describing the role of the pastor and the relationship of the pastor to the congregation? Ministers, like other professionals, tend to think in

terms of professional specialized functions (preaching, counseling, education, administration, denominational responsibilities, etc.). Lay persons tend to think in relational terms and to describe the minister and his work in personal and pastoral terms.

6. What is the definition of "interchurch cooperation"? Pastors often describe as interchurch cooperation events and activities arranged by the clergy and attended by lay persons. The laity tend to think of interchurch cooperation as activities and programs planned and implemented with a high degree of lay involvement by members from two or more congregations.

7. What is the meaning of the word *stewardship?* Ministers tend to think in terms of sharing of time, talent, energy, leadership, and money. Lay leaders tend to think of stewardship as being synonymous with "money raising" or "pledging the budget."

8. Should the denomination speak out on social issues? Clergy tend to be more strongly supportive than the laity of the right and obligation of the denomination to speak out on social issues. [3]

9. Who is the more judgmental and arbitrary? Clergy tend to be far more accepting of diversity and ambiguity than do the laity. The laity tend to be far less tolerant, and to classify people and situations in very arbitrary terms more easily than do the clergy. [4]

10. How important is pastoral calling? This is one of the most divisive issues in literally hundreds of congregations. In general the laity tend to put pastoral calling on members in their homes in the top third of the priorities for how a minister allocates his time. Ministers tend to place routine "friendly" calling in the middle or bottom of the priorities for the pastor's time. [5]

It would be easy to list another dozen areas in which the laity and the clergy tend to differ in their perspectives, but it is not necessary to detail. It is important, however, that when they are seated around the same decision-making table both clergy and laity should remember that they do not speak from the same frame of reference.

When Were You Born?

"Anyone here care for an extra doughnut?" inquired a clean-shaven, prosperous-looking man in his fifties with a crew cut and wearing a yellow sports shirt. He had stopped in at the small roadside diner in Kansas at midmorning for a cup of coffee and a couple of doughnuts. When no one spoke he added, "I finished breakfast less than two hours ago and I simply don't have room for this doughnut. Are you sure none of you care for it?" When no one responded, he wrapped it up in a napkin, paid his check, and walked out to his car carrying the doughnut in his hand.

After he had left, a woman in her middle twenties said to her husband and to anyone else who cared to listen, "Now there's a clear example of what my sociology teacher described as 'the depression ethic.' I'll bet that poor fellow grew up during the depression when his parents really had to struggle to have enough food on the table for the family. No one else in here looks to be past thirty. We couldn't understand why he was so concerned about letting one doughnut be thrown in the garbage, and I'm sure he can't understand why no one here jumped at his offer of free food. There's more than a generation gap here—there's a vast difference in perspective."

One of the most influential factors affecting the frame of reference each person brings to a question or problem is the experiences of his youth and his formative years.

When the leaders at Immanuel Church first began to discuss construction of a new church school wing in 1964 there was a division between those who wanted to go ahead with the construction as soon as possible and those who wanted to wait a few years until the money in the building fund could cover most of the costs. All but three of the persons in the group that was eager to act had been born after 1926, and one of their major arguments was, "It will be very difficult to raise money until people can actually see that this project, which has been in the 'talk stage' for fifteen years, is real. The easiest time to raise money for a building fund is during construction when there is a lot of excitement because people can see something happening."

Every member of the group that wanted to have most of the money in hand before beginning construction had been born before 1920. They urged caution, and one of them warned, "Many of you don't remember this, but we started construction on the first unit here in 1929. The contractor went bankrupt about the time he was finishing the basement and we lost all of the advance money we had paid to him to buy material. We met in the basement here from 1930 to 1946, when we finally were able to complete the sanctuary. We were luckier than some, at that, because we were always able to pay our creditors. The Methodists over there finished their building in 1928 with a big mortgage and ended up paying off their creditors with twenty-five cents on the dollar. That Lutheran church on the corner finished construction in 1930. The insurance company which held the mortgage took title to the property in 1932, and the Lutherans had to rent their own church back from the insurance company until 1939, when they were able to repurchase it. We had better wait until we have at least one-half of the anticipated cost in hand before we start construction." The frame of reference of the person who lived through the Great Depression as an adult is different from that of the person who did not know the depression from an adult perspective.

The frame of reference of the person who was born in 1922 and served in World War II is different from the frame of reference of the person who was born in 1948 and resisted being drafted to serve in the Vietnam conflict.

The frame of reference of the woman who was born in 1910 and accepts the role of women in American society is different from the frame of reference of the woman who was born in 1950 and questions the way women have been treated in American society.

The frame of reference of the black man born in Georgia in 1918 who served in a segregated military unit in World War II tends to be different from the frame of reference of the black man born in Georgia in 1948 who served in a biracial unit in Vietnam.

While the year of birth and the impact of the formative years tend to have a profound influence on the frame of reference a person uses in looking at a specific issue, they are not the only factors, and much is relative. In 1960 John F. Kennedy was regarded as young. After all, at age forty three, he was the youngest person ever elected as President of the United States. A few years later George Blanda, also aged forty-three, was regarded as old. He was the oldest player ever to be named the most valuable player in the American Football Conference.

What About Original Sin?

Perhaps the most significant watershed that is apparent when we review the impact of an individual's frame of reference on his expectations and decisions is the doctrine of original sin. Traditionally conservatives, from Edmund Burke to James Burnham to Edward Banfield, have based their interpretations of contemporary reality on an acceptance of the doctrine that man is partly corrupt and is limited in his potential. Traditionally liberals, from Jean Jacques Rousseau to John Stuart Mill to Thomas Jefferson to Hubert Humphrey, have argued that man is inherently good, capable of a rational approach to the world around him, and able to solve the problems which the conservatives assert are a natural result of the sinful nature of man.[6]

In recent years this debate has usually centered not on the subject of original sin directly, but rather on specific problems such as substandard housing, poverty, the quality of the public schools, racial discrimination, and equality.[7] However, whenever a Daniel Patrick Moynihan or an R. J. Herrnstein or a

Frederick Mosteller or a Christopher Jencks or a James S. Coleman or a David Armor or an Edward Banfield suggests that perfection may not be attainable, the debate tends to shift back to ideological positions which represent differences in the frame of reference used in looking at man and the environment.

Walter Lippmann emphasized a refinement in this debate when he described the 1972 presidential election as a repudiation of the Rousseauistic philosophy that man is essentially good. Lippmann's basic point is that in every advanced modern industrial society there comes a time when the people conclude that it is impossible for the government to bring out the perfect man by creation of a perfect environment through governmental action. Lippmann argues that the fundamental difference between what he describes as a "Jacobin revolutionary philosophy" and "Lyndon Johnson liberalism" is that the former views man as perfectable, while the latter views man as "an improvable but not perfectable." [8] This concept of a threefold division into "Jacobin revolutionary," liberal, and conservative may be more comfortable than the old twofold one to many who are attempting to develop a frame of reference that is helpful in the last quarter of the twentieth century.

During every generation in recent American history the churches have been torn by a conflict that attempted to lock both the clergy and the laity into a "conservative" or a "liberal" stance, with the doctrine of original sin as the basic point of cleavage, although it was seldom identified in these terms. Lippmann's argument has much to commend it. It helps to explain contemporary reality. It helps to explain, at least in part, why many people tend to become more "conservative" as they grow older, or, to be more precise, why as they grow older and become less sure of the perfectability of man, many people tend to appear more "conservative" to younger "liberals" and "radicals."

The Christian, however, should not allow himself to be locked into the liberal-conservative dichotomy. The central thesis of the orthodox Christian faith denies both of these overly simplified explanations of reality. While Christianity affirms the doctrine of original sin, this does not leave man in a hopeless position. On the other hand, the breaking of the chains of sin has not been left to man alone. God, in the person of Jesus Christ, came into the world to redeem man. This is the fact that has been celebrated around the world on every Easter Sunday for centuries.[9]

Thus the Christian brings to every discussion of change a distinctive frame of reference which distinguishes him from the humanist, who comes with a more simplified "liberal" or "conservative" set of assumptions about the implications of the doctrine of original sin. It may be that a new Reinhold Niebuhr, someone born after 1945 who can achieve a sense of identification with the post–World War II generation, will emerge in the 1970s or 1980s to help Christians clarify their frame of reference on this issue of original sin.

What About the Holy Spirit?

Closely related to the issue of the doctrine of original sin is the question of the impact of the Holy Spirit on the decision-making process.

One test of the perceived influence of the Holy Spirit in making decisions within individual congregations is to review the results to this question asked of slightly over 1,300 congregational leaders: "You have 100 points to distribute among what you see as the most influential factors in how decisions are made in this congregation. Allocate the appropriate number of points to each influence or factor. Make sure the total is exactly 100." Following this will be a list of six to twenty factors, tailored to reflect the distinctive characteristics of that congregation.[10] A sheet of paper with the instructions and the appropriate factors listed on it is given to each of the leaders in the congregation. In a small church this included 8 leaders, and in a larger congregation nearly 100 persons filled out the sheet. The sheets are collected and a composite score is calculated for that congregation. After the question had been used with over three dozen congregations the degree of diversity in the responses was analyzed. In each case two of the factors on the list were "the Holy Spirit" and "Goals." In only one of the thirty-six did the composite score for the influence of the Holy Spirit exceed 10 percent. In a majority of these congregations a larger composite score was received by such influences as the minister, tradition, the governing board, the program, financial limitations, and an adult Sunday School class.

It appears that this picture is changing, however, and a new recognition of the power of the Holy Spirit is being perceived in a rapidly growing number of churches in the United States, including both Roman Catholic and Protestant. In many congregations the operational version of the Holy Trinity is being redefined from God, Jesus, and the Bible, or God, Jesus, and Mary, to God, Jesus, and the Holy Spirit. This may be the most important change in the decision-making processes of American churches in the twentieth century!

Commitment and the Church

"Our problem here at North Street Church is that our people aren't committed!" a fifty-five-year-old member of that congregation declared to a visiting denominational staff member. She spoke with obvious conviction and continued, "You can be a tremendous help to us here and make this a really important night in the life of this congregation if you can tell us how to make our people more committed!"

The denominational staff person had been invited out to meet with fifteen leaders from the North Street congregation to help them define and respond to several questions that were facing this 400-member church. There were only eight lay persons and the minister present for this first meeting. Several of those present affirmed that they too believed a lack of commitment was the source of most of their problems. One person declared, "Back in 1954 I joined this congregation because I was so impressed by the commitment of the people.

53

We've moved twice since then, and we now drive seventeen miles each way two or three times a week to get here. I think that indicates our concern. But half of the members here don't seem to care whether this church lives or dies. If you can help us get people to be more committed we'll be able to solve all of the other problems."

What is the appropriate frame of reference for the denominational staff person to use in responding to this request?

One alternative would be for him to encourage those present to think the issue through and to improve their own awareness by asking questions of those present: "Why do you believe people are committed?" "Why do you believe the level of commitment in this congregation has changed over the years?" "What do you understand to be the basis for the commitment of each person here tonight?" "How do people become more committed?" "How has the depth of your commitment changed in recent years?"

A second alternative would be for him to affirm the importance of the issue and to shift to an experienced learning or action-reflection frame of reference. Thus he might respond by saying, "This is a very important issue, and perhaps we should spend some time on it before we take up any other issue. First, let's make a list of twenty or so persons we know in this community who are clearly committed to some cause or issue or organization, and interview them. After we have each interviewed two from this list about their commitment, we can come back here two weeks from tonight and reflect on what we have learned about commitment and what we can do to help deepen the commitment of the members of this parish." The list of those to be interviewed might include a doctor who works eighty hours a week, a person who is a very active leader in the civil rights movement, a teacher, a baseball fan, an active political leader, a minister from another church, a lay leader from a different congregation, an active leader in the women's liberation movement, a labor leader, a Boy Scout leader, the president of a local service club, a mother, the football coach in the high school, two or three members of the group present that evening at North Street Church, and a dozen other persons who display a firm commitment to some value, organization, ideal, or institution.

A third alternative would be for the visiting staff person to help the people present that evening develop a more systematic frame of reference for looking at commitment, which distinguishes (*a*) between a commitment to God and a commitment to a church and (*b*) between a commitment to a shared heritage and a commitment to contemporary goals.

During the centuries since the founding of the Christian church a tendency has developed to equate confessing Jesus Christ as Lord and Savior with membership in a congregation of worshiping Christians. While some may find it difficult to understand or defend their point of view, there are many persons who do identify themselves as Christians, but who are not members of a worshiping congregation. Others are members, but do not participate actively in the life of any congregation.

This fact of life suggests that it may be helpful to distinguish between the commitment of the individual to Christ as Savior and the commitment of the individual to that institutional expression of the universal Christian church identified as the worshiping congregation. Furthermore it may be helpful to distinguish between the *motivation* for commitment and the *expression* of commitment in examining the relationship of individuals to a particular congregation. It appears that most of the *active* members of the typical congregation express their commitment to that congregation in one of two ways. In each case the expression of commitment becomes a motivating factor in the actions and responses of church members.

In some congregations that have been established for a decade or longer, the commitment of individuals to the congregation appears to be based to a very substantial degree on a heritage shared by many of the members. The group of most deeply committed members includes some, but not necessarily all, of those who have spent a large proportion of their adult lives as members of the same congregation and/or have not spent many years as active members of other congregations. It also includes the adult offspring of such members. In the typical example of this pattern, the congregation was established at least forty years ago, many of the active adult members of today have been members of this congregation for at least three decades, and only a small proportion of the older adults have spent as many adult years in another congregation as they have in this one. These individual members share many of the same roots in the congregation. They have shared many responsibilities together. They have been through "good" and "bad" times together. They have been very close to one another and have a strong attachment to the congregation. In many congregations like this most of the older members share the same national, racial, subcultural, socio-economic-educational, linguistic, and/or theological characteristics.

The other most frequently encountered expression of active commitment by individuals to a particular congregation is in shared contemporary goals. These active members tend to focus their conversation about "our church" on what is happening now. The emphasis on shared contemporary goals is often expressed orally in such comments as "It looks like we'll be able to move into the new building in another month," or "Our weekday nursery school now has over thirty children in it," or "We raised over $3,000 last Sunday in the special offering for World Missions," or "Our high school youth group will be going to Haiti next month to help expand a children's TB hospital," or "We have more than fifty trained lay persons in our visitation-evangelism program," or "Our lay witness mission is scheduled for next month," or "Let me share with you what's happening in our new Bible study group," or "We had considerable opposition, but we helped launch the planned parenthood clinic which is housed in our building," or "We seem to be starting a new growth group here every month."

The first point to recognize in looking at these two different expressions of commitment to the church is that when *neither* is operative the congregation tends to appear to be disorganized and to reflect feelings of apathy, despair, and pessimism.

The second point to recognize in looking at these alternative expressions of commitment by individuals to a particular congregation is that often it is counterproductive to label either one as "good" or "bad." It is much more productive to reflect on the implications of each for the attitudes and behavior patterns of members.

Third, these two expressions of commitment should not be identified as "active" or "passive." The member with a commitment to the congregation based largely on a shared heritage may be expressing that commitment in a very active manner. Likewise the person with a commitment based largely on shared contemporary goals may be only passively or vicariously involved in the actual implementation of those goals.

Fourth, this frame of reference may offer some clue for the reason behind the inactivity or apathy or indifference of many members who are considered to be "inactive" or "nonparticipating." How many of the inactive members feel a sense of an important shared heritage in this congregation? How many of the inactive members reflect strong interest or a sense of ownership of the contemporary goals of this congregation?

Fifth, a sense of shared roots and an involvement (either active or passive) in the contemporary goals of a congregation are not incompatible. Many individual members express their commitment to their congregation *both* ways. In scores of congregations members who explain why they are members of that particular called-out community of Christians in terms of shared roots are actively involved in formulating and implementing new goals for the congregation to use in responding to the call to faithfulness and obedience.

Many congregations intentionally and creatively reinforce the sense of a shared heritage and also emphasize a broad base of ownership in the contemporary goals of the church.

Sixth, unless care is exercised, however, these two different expressions of commitment by members to the same congregation can become a divisive force between those who are viewed by others as the conservators of tradition and of "but this is the way we've always done it here" and those who are viewed as proponents of change. This is often a major source of the bickering which inhibits ministry.

Seventh, this frame of reference for looking at commitment by individuals to a particular congregation opens up possibilities for planning for future ministry. It is often possible to build new goals in ministry on old traditions and to involve in the formulation and implementation of new goals the people who trace their basic commitment to that church back to a shared heritage.

Eighth, congregations where the commitment of most members to the church is based largely on shared roots often have these characteristics too: a better-than-average level of giving, many women over 50 who have been together in *this* church for over 30 years, a self-image of being a conservative or evangelical congregation, at least two or three strong adult Sunday School classes or other groups in which the members have a deep loyalty to that class, several three- or four-generation families, an expectation that the youth and young adults of today are the leaders of *this* congregation of tomorrow, an above-average resistance to change, a large number of very loyal older women, several adults under 65 who have "retired" from active leadership roles in the church, relatively few persons aged 20–40 not related by blood or marriage to other members, three or four vigorous and able women leaders in the 30–45 age range who are daughters of members, an emphasis in the outreach of the congregation on "what people ought to do" rather than on the self-identified needs of people, a strong but shrinking women's organization, and a statistical record filled with a series of numbers getting smaller with the passage of time.

Ninth, the congregation where most of the members' commitment to the church is based on shared goals frequently also has the following characteristics: easy assimilation of new members into the life and fellowship of the congregation, a broad and varied program, very few third-generation members, a strong emphasis on "results" and accountability, a record of some members leaving in protest, dependence on designated giving to supplement the regular level of giving to the unified budget, the highly visible presence of several members with a contagious enthusiasm for "what our church is doing in ministry," a shared style of leadership, clearly understood staff responsibilities, an above-average turnover in membership, very few leaders, if any, who refer to this as a "Sunday morning" church, and the median age of the members under 55 and usually under 50.

Finally, lest anyone misunderstand, this is not an attempt to "prove" a cause-and-effect relationship, but only to describe two types of churches that are encountered frequently and to suggest that the type of church may be related to the expression of commitment by members to their church.

It helps the leaders as they plan for the future to understand themselves in terms of the primary expression of the commitment of the members to the congregation.

Types of Churches

As suggested above, it is often helpful in planning for the mission and ministry of a congregation to develop a frame of reference based on the type of church involved. One obvious example is the congregation in which the most common basis of commitment by individuals to that congregation is from a shared heritage. Another is the long-established, small country church. A third is old First Church downtown. A fourth is the suburban mission founded twelve to fifteen years ago that still has not reached the size and institutional strength that enables it both to be financially self supporting and to have a full-time pastor.[11] The use of a frame of reference of this type is helpful in clarifying expectations, predicting normative patterns, and raising questions that help distinguish symptoms from problems. It is a far more useful frame of reference than simply talking about "large" congregations or "small" congregations, both of which are subjective terms.

How Large Is Small?

"The future certainly looks bright for our church," commented John Brant, a member of Trinity Church. "We're getting to be a big church. At Easter there were over 250 in church, and we have about 160 to 170 on the average Sunday. That's up from a year ago when 150 was a big crowd."

"I wish I could say the same for our parish," replied his friend Tom Dean as they ate lunch together. "At Calvary we used to really pack them in. A dozen years ago we never had fewer than 300 in church on Sunday morning, and on many days we would go over 400. Now we average just a shade over 200."

How large is a church that averages 200 at worship on Sunday morning? From John Brant's perspective that is a very impressive size. From the perspective of his friend Tom Dean, 200 at worship on Sunday morning is a figure that produces gloom rather than rejoicing.

This again illustrates the influence of the mental "baggage" each person carries or the frame of reference he or she uses to analyze a specific situation.

One example of how the frame of reference influences the decision-making process in the churches is the many proposals by denominational and interdenominational executives and staff members to encourage the consolidation or closing of "small" churches.

What is the size of a "small" church? One response to this question is from the perspective of the minister or lay person who has always been associated with "large" congregations. From the perspective of these individuals a "small" congregation may be one with fewer than 200 members, or one which averages fewer than 75 or 80 people at worship on Sunday morning. Some persons who have always been associated with very large congregations may think of any congregation with fewer than 300 to 400 members as "small."

A second response is to reflect on the number of associations in American society which have more than 100 members in the local groups. How many service clubs such as the Lions, the Rotary Club, or the Kiwanis have as many as 100 members? How many adult education groups have as many as 50 members? How many Boy Scout troops or Cub Scout packs have as many as 60 members? How many 4H clubs have as many as 40 members? How many hobby or special interest clubs have as many as 100 members? (See "The Rule of Forty" below.)

A third response to the question "How large is a small church?" is to look at the statistical record. Sixty percent of the congregations in the Church of the Brethren have fewer than 150 members. Almost exactly half of the congregations in The United Presbyterian Church in the U.S.A. have fewer than 200 members. (In 1972 the smallest congregation in the UPCUSA had one member.) Approximately half of the congregations in The United Methodist Church have fewer than 150 members. Half of all churches in America have an average attendance at Sunday morning worship of fewer than 80, and a quarter average fewer than 40.

Proposals for the consolidation or closing of "small" congregations must be evaluated in terms of the definition of "small." This definition tends to reflect the frame of reference of the person offering the definition. This again illustrates the value of clarifying the basic assumptions or the frame of reference a participant brings to the decision-making process.

The Rule of Forty

Closely related to this is a concept that can be described simply as "the rule of forty." Based on observations of human behavior patterns, the rule of forty is derived from the many occasions when forty appears to be the maximum number of units that one person can manage effectively. A few examples will illustrate this point. Specialists in management science suggest that when the number of events in a PERT (Program Evaluation and Review Techniques) diagram exceeds forty, it is necessary to use a computer to locate the critical path for scheduling the chain of activities. There is almost universal agreement among educators that the absolute maximum number of pupils for one classroom teacher is forty. While the number has varied over the years, the maximum number of players permitted on a major league football squad has been forty in most seasons. Several religious groups, such as some branches of the Amish, divide into two congregations when the number of families passes forty.

In general, when human beings gather into voluntary associations, whether it be to form a service club or the local of a labor union or an athletic squad, or to divide into classes for educational experiences, or to form a Scout troop, or to organize a military unit around platoons, the maximum size tends to be under forty. This may be a useful frame of reference for looking at the size of a congregation and the number of groups within the congregation.

These are only a few examples to show how the frame of reference influences the decision-making process in the churches. Many more could be cited, such as the differences in the perspective of the United Methodist district superintendent between when he is functioning as a member of the cabinet and when he is out in the district, or the differences in perspective between the minister seeking to leave his present pastorate and the denominational placement official concerned with helping the pulpit committee find the "right" minister, or the differences in perspective between the person who describes the glass as being half-full and the person who describes the same glass as being half-empty.

It is difficult to overemphasize the significance of the frames of reference of both the writer and the reader as this discussion moves on to examine the pressures on religious institutions and organizations in general, and on denominational structures in particular.

3 The Pressures of Institutionalism

In 1964 a master plan for theological education in the Lutheran Church in America recommended unification of the denomination's two seminaries in Pennsylvania. Previous discussions directed toward the merger of the two schools and the work that produced the master plan had revealed the weaknesses and the strengths of each seminary. How did the two schools respond to the 1964 recommendation for unification? In exactly the same way that they had responded to earlier proposals to unite the two schools. Each one "set itself on a course to strengthen its bargaining power." [1]

The 1964 General Conference of The Methodist Church provided the necessary approval for the denomination to proceed with plans to unite with The Evangelical United Brethren Church. The two denominations held special sessions of their General Conferences in Chicago in November, 1966, at which the critical votes on unification were taken. The consummation of the merger of these two denominations took place in April, 1968. Since both denominations had seminaries in the Chicago metropolitan area it appeared to many observers that the smaller of the two, the Evangelical Theological Seminary in Naperville, would (1) move west, (2) merge with another seminary in another state, or (3) unite with Garrett Theological Seminary, the Methodist seminary which is located next to Northwestern University in Evanston, just north of Chicago. Construction of a new academic building on the Naperville campus was completed in the fall of 1967, over a year after the critical vote in favor of merger had been taken. At the same time the Naperville school, for the first time in its history, hired an admissions counselor to go out and recruit students.

卍

The leaders at Immanuel Church had invited the person specializing in evangelism on the synod staff to meet with them one evening. When he arrived and began to question them on their concerns, they replied that they needed professional help in developing a more effective evangelism program. "I'm the chairman of our evangelism committee," explained one member, "and I have to confess that we have only met once a year for the past two years that I have been chairman. The only thing we accomplished at either of those meetings was to prepare a one-paragraph statement for our report to the annual meeting. We need help in developing an effective program to evangelize this neighborhood, and we hope you can help us develop one that will work." After several more minutes of discussion, another person, who had not spoken previously, blurted out, "Let's be honest about this! Last month we learned that the slate roof on the church is in very bad shape and it will cost us at least $35,000 for that and other repairs. What we're really talking about is how do we get some more members to help us pay our bills? We're down to fewer than three hundred members, compared to over fourteen hundred twenty years ago, and there are just too few of us to maintain this big old building. If we don't get some help soon, we'll have to close!"

卍

In each of these three incidents the behavior of the people involved in the decision-making processes was completely natural, normal, and predictable. In each of these three incidents the influence of institutional pressures is highly visible. In each of these three incidents the first law of institutional behavior is illustrated very clearly.

Anyone seriously interested in analyzing the behavior of religious organizations, in understanding how decisions are made in the churches, or in predicting the responses of the churches to future questions would be well advised to consider two statements. The first is that religious organizations tend to behave like other institutions and organizations rather than to display a distinctive *religious* emphasis in making decisions.[2] The second is that the responses and behavior of institutions are predictable.

Both of these basic points can be illustrated by listing a dozen of the forms in which institutional pressures influence the decision-making processes of organizations.

Forms of Institutional Pressure

1. Institutional self-preservation usually has a major influence on, and often dominates, the decision-making processes of an organization.

This basic law was illustrated by the three incidents described at the beginning of this chapter. Further illustrations are the continued existence of the March of Dimes long after polio was eliminated, and the church which agreed that the confirmation age should be raised from thirteen to fourteen, but postponed implementation for an extra year "because a lot of our members are moving out of the community this year, and if we don't have a confirmation class this year, the record will show a net loss for our membership figure at the end of the year."

2. Institutions tend to become client-centered very quickly.

The location for a new hospital is selected because there is no hospital in that part of the county. Within a few years the operation of the hospital is oriented to serving patients, without regard to place of residence, rather than to serving nearby residents.

A new mission is started in a suburban community to reach the people moving in who might otherwise have no active church affiliation. Within a few years the congregation is large enough to become self-sufficient. The schedule, program, and allocation of the pastor's time are planned primarily to service the members, rather than to reach other newcomers who have no active church affiliation.[3]

3. The original purpose of a nonprofit organization is soon subverted to give first priority to the needs, preferences, and convenience of the professional staff rather than to the clientele.

This is illustrated by the schedules and operation of schools, libraries, hospitals, and agencies to serve the handicapped.[4] It is illustrated by the church with a part-time secretary which schedules both the minister and the secretary to be in the building in the mornings instead of scheduling the secretary to work afternoons so that the church will be open all day and there will always be someone there to answer the telephone. It is illustrated by the dozens of United Methodist annual conferences which in the allocation of financial receipts give top priority to pensions for ministers, and a lower priority to foreign missions.

4. The purpose and the output or product of an organization are often not the same thing.

This basic generalization is illustrated by the following examples. A manufacturing corporation was created to make a profit for the stockholders, and policy decisions are influenced by the probable impact on profits; but the output of the factory is employment opportunities, air pollution, and automobiles. An adult Sunday School class was formed for educational purposes, but its major product is fellowship. A denominational publishing house was created for the purpose of producing publications for the denomination, but the output by which many people evaluate it is the profit for the denominational pension system.

Though there is a temptation to evaluate an organization on criteria derived from its statement of purpose, often the most useful evaluation is on the basis of the output or product.

5. The normal sequence in an organization is from charisma to bureaucracy.

Most denominations and many congregations were established by charismatic personalities. Among the names in this long list of influential leaders are Martin Luther, John Wesley,

John Calvin, Gilbert Tennent, George Whitefield, Theodore J. Frelinghuysen, Jonathan Edwards, Henry Melchior Mühlenberg, Samuel S. Schmucker, Burton W. Stone, Alexander Campbell, Menno Simons, Samuel Seabury, C. F. W. Walther, Francis Asbury, Count Zinzendorf, Philip William Otterbein, James McGready, and Franklin Clark Fry.

Each of these individuals helped establish what today can be described as an institutionalized bureaucracy. This is not to suggest that they failed. Their names are mentioned only to illustrate that the churches are not immune to the pattern of development from an individual, to a movement, which eventually emerges as a legitimate institution. There are many sources of legitimacy for an institution, including longevity (after any institution has been around for a sufficient period of time it becomes accepted as legitimate, regardless of how it fulfills the purpose for which it was originally founded); impressive symbols (buildings, rituals, etc.); positive benefits (delivering services to its clientele which they value); mystery (no one understands it, but no one is willing to challenge it); and charismatic leadership. Since charismatic leadership is highly vulnerable to the passage of time, eventually it becomes necessary to seek other means of legitimatizing and perpetuating the institution. The creation of a bureaucracy which provides for the location of authority, the division of work, and the allocation of resources is a normal response to the impact of the passage of time.

6. Few individuals can participate effectively on more than two levels of institutional structure.

This explains why a mayor may be a leader in the state league of municipalities and in the regional association of cities, but does not have the time and energy to be involved in the national activities of his political party.

It explains why the pastor who is heavily involved in the local council of churches and in a national denominational board seldom has the time and energy to be heavily involved in the regional judicatory. It also explains why that layman who is on the executive committee of the synod and on a national denominational board is no longer an active leader in his own parish.

7. Vertical relationships dominate institutional relationships.

This generalization explains why most pastors know a larger number of ministers in their synod or conference or diocese than they know in the county where their church is located.

It partially explains why community, metropolitan, and state councils of churches, which are organized on a system of horizontal institutional relationships, have built-in difficulties.

It also helps explain why all institutions are having difficulty abandoning a hierarchical organizational structure.

8. Every organization seeks to enhance its own institutional and economic security.

This generalization helps to explain why many congregations have so many separate treasuries—one for the woman's organization, one for each circle, one for the church school, one for each of the four adult Sunday School classes, one for the youth group, and one for the congregation as a whole.

9. Every organization seeks to be free from accountability to any other organization.

This generalization helps to explain why many church-related colleges, seminaries, hospitals, and homes strive to have an independent and self-perpetuating governing board rather than have the members of the board elected by the parent denomination.

It helps explain the generations of tension between the pastor and the governing body of the congregation and (a) the Sunday School and (b) the women's organization.

It is the basic *institutional* motivation for a congregational polity in church government.

This generalization also helps explain the three-level system of church organization (congregation, regional judicatory, national denominational body) of the United Church of Christ and of the Christian Church (Disciples of Christ) in which each of the three levels is an autonomous unit.

10. Institutional considerations are normally far more influential than theological or philosophical considerations whenever changes in the institutional structure or the allocation of resources are being considered.

Efforts in recent years to unite two or more denominations have usually involved a group of members who insisted that the basic emphasis in the merger negotiations should be on the "renewal" of the church.

In commenting on this subject James M. Wall described an institutional group which he saw as acting primarily from a functional orientation. Their emphasis is on a pragmatic evaluation of any merger proposal based on whether it would improve the functioning of the church. At the other pole he described a theological group composed of those who are acting primarily from a biblical-theological orientation and asking "why" questions in contrast to the "how" questions of the institutional group.[5]

This same pattern of the dominance of institutional pressures is reflected in the budget of nearly every congregation and denomination where institutional maintenance has priority over program and ministry.

The same pattern is also reflected in proposals for the merger of two congregations where far more attention is directed to questions such as which building will be the meeting place of the new merged congregation, or who will be the pastor, or the name of the new congregation, than to the theological considerations which encourage or discourage unity.

11. Policy formation, goals formulation, and the allocation of resources in every organization tend to be influenced more by the full-time professional staff than by the volunteers in policy-making positions.

This is a perfectly obvious point, yet the churches are filled with people who prefer to play a game of "buck passing" in which the professional staff avoid difficult questions by replying, "I am unable to say now what we will do. Our board does not meet until the first of next month, and I cannot predict what action they will take on this matter."

The "executive secretary" of any organization, whether it be the pastor of a church, the chief executive of a national board, a seminary dean, the executive of a regional judicatory, or the executive officer of a council of churches, who consistently offers this response to questions *and who believes what he says*, should be dismissed for administrative incompetence.

12. The normal result of pressures is resistance to change and preservation of the status quo.

In all organizations the "safe" response to change is an attempt to maintain the status quo. Criticism is more likely to be evoked by change than by indecision and inaction.

One widespread example of this is the many congregations, denominational agencies, theological seminaries, and councils of churches that have attempted to preserve the status quo as long as possible. A common result has been the gradual elimination, owing to the passage of time and changing circumstances, of many alternatives which were more attractive than the options that are left when it is no longer possible to perpetuate the past. Finally a decision for change must be made, and it is made amid a rash of regret-filled comments about "what might have been if we had acted sooner."

The larger or more complex the organization, the longer it has been in operation, or the longer the tenure of the key decision-makers, the more likely it is that these and other institutional pressures will dominate the decision-making processes.

This is one of the reasons why organizations periodically feel the need to "bring in new blood" or to "restructure." An eternal hope of the proponents of "fresh leadership" or of restructure is that one of the results will be a reduction in institutional pressures.

It is also one of the reasons why most calls for new leadership or for restructure include pleas for a "more efficient" operation or a "simpler" organizational structure.

It may be tempting for the critic of ecclesiastical organizations to interpret these twelve generalizations as criticisms. That would be a complete misreading of the intent behind the presentation of this list. The twelve generalizations are presented in a completely neutral descriptive context. They are offered simply as generalizations which help explain why institutional pressures are so influential in the decision-making processes of the churches. They are not offered as a comprehensive or exhaustive listing, only as a means of suggesting to the serious student of the decision-making processes in the churches that institutional pressures are real, that they can be defined, and that their impact can be predicted.

Many critics of the institutional expressions of the universal church do not realize that these institutional pressures are normative in every complex organization. Instead they tend to see specific manifestations of institutional pressures in a particular organization as a factor which must be completely eliminated. Frequently it is proposed that these institutional pressures can be eliminated by a "renewal" of the organization, by "getting back to the Bible," by developing an "ecumenical stance," by merger with another ecclesiastical organization, by replacing the present staff, by restructure, by reducing the budget, or by some other equally naïve and simplistic approach. Institutional pressures can be reduced. They cannot be eliminated.

If the church is to be effective in a world filled with institutions, it must be present in several institutional expressions of the universal church. Whenever and wherever this occurs, the decision-making processes will be vulnerable in varying degrees to many institutional pressures, a few of which have been identified in the preceding pages.

In Defense of Denominationalism

One of the institutional expressions of the universal church becomes visible when several congregations constitute what is usually referred to as a denomination. Throughout the history of the Christian churches in the United States denominations have been subjected to considerable criticism. They have been accused of being unnecessary; of representing a subversion of the goals of the Christian faith; of being a barrier to unity; of preventing the reform of society; of inhibiting the building of the Kingdom of God; and of being a source of distrust and bigotry, a barrier to effective evangelism, and a major obstacle to the achievement of a long list of other cherished dreams. The length and the variety of the list of criticisms, of which this is only an excerpt, suggest that the denominations have tremendous power.

A more creative approach to the place of denominations, and their role in the decision-making processes of the churches, would be to begin to look at them as voluntary associations.

Voluntary associations of human beings tend to be gathered around one or both of two principles. The first is association as the result of a shared commitment. The second is association as the result of a legal covenant and a set of formal rules. Whenever a schism occurs in a religious organization and the dispute is taken into court, these two opposing concepts become highly visible. Every year an average of two dozen new appellate decisions are filed in the law reports on intrachurch quarrels. Usually the dispute in court centers on control of the property. Should the church be seen as a voluntary association bound together by commitment to a doctrine or creed? If the answer is in the affirmative, the property goes to the group which is true to the creed. Or should it be perceived by the secular courts as a voluntary association bound together by a set of formal rules (polity)? If the answer to this question is in the affirmative, the property should go to the party which has been in accord with the polity of that church.[6] In recent years this fact of denominational life has become highly visible in the Presbyterian Church in the U.S., where both doctrine and a connectional polity are stressed.

There are many additional reasons why churches tend to cluster into denominations. In his pioneering book on the origins of denominationalism, H. Richard Niebuhr concluded that any effort to distinguish denominations by references to doctrine or theology was artificial. He identified the Anabaptists, the Quakers, the English Methodists, and The Salvation Army as examples of denominations of "the disinherited," while the Calvinists, Lutherans, and Christian Scientists stand as examples of what Niebuhr termed "the churches of the middle class," and the Baptists, the Disciples of Christ, and American Methodism are examples of churches of "frontier religion." [7] In examining the sources of denominationalism both Niebuhr and Robert Lee[8] were concerned primarily with the twin issues of unity and disunity.

If the perspective is shifted from the historical and social reasons behind the emergence of denominations to a pragmatic and operational focus, the nature of the debate is changed. Instead of focusing on the merits of unity and the evils of disunity, the discussion shifts to institutional and organizational questions. To state it more bluntly, it is a meaningless diversion to spend scarce resources on such questions as whether denominations are good or bad or whether it would be better to eliminate all existing denominations and replace them with one larger denomination which would be defined as the "united church." (Inasmuch as several denominations, including Methodists, Presbyterians, Pentecostals, Lutherans, and others, now use the word "united" as part of their name, it appears questionable whether use of that word in the title of a denomination influences its performance.)

It may be more productive to discuss such questions as these: What does a denomination do? How can it do what it is doing more effectively? What else should it be doing? What is it doing that it might be wise to discontinue? How does its present organization and decision-making structure affect its capability to carry out its performance?

Denominations do carry many responsibilities that individual congregations either cannot accomplish or else cannot accomplish as effectively. Denominations provide for the theological training of ministers; maintain a network of communication for church members; enable the churches to be more effective in ministry on issues; offer opportunities for a public Christian witness; provide additional channels for the churches to fulfill their prophetic role; develop, mobilize, and make available resources for individuals and for congregations; organize new worshiping congregations; offer in-service training opportunities; provide a range of growth experiences for individuals and groups; provide channels for individuals and congregations to be involved in missionary and missional ventures not available through most congregations unilaterally; develop and enforce standards of membership; provide pension programs for professional church workers; offer counsel for congregations and pastors; increase the vocational mobility of the clergy; assist congregations in personnel recruitment; and enable people and congregations to see themselves, and to function, as a part of the universal church.[9]

This is not offered as a complete list of what denominations do, but rather to suggest that if present denominational structures were eliminated the churches would very quickly replace them with an organizational structure for accomplishing these same tasks. In today's institutional climate it is possible that some of these tasks would be "contracted out" to nondenominational agencies, but the organizational growth of the younger and faster-growing denominational bodies suggests that the list of contracted-out tasks would probably be a short one, whose content and length would probably be influenced more by financial limitations than by ideological considerations.

From a review of this list of denominational tasks it is clear that some denominational structures are more effective than others in carrying out certain responsibilities. For example, the appointive system of ministerial placement in The United Methodist Church is more effective than the ministerial placement systems of the Presbyterians, the Lutherans, the Disciples of Christ, the United Church of Christ, the Episcopalians, or the Quakers in enhancing the mobility of the clergy in general and of those who have passed their fiftieth birthday in particular.

This illustration introduces another concept that must be considered in any discussion of the institutional character of denominations and of the decision-making processes in denominations. It can be described under the generalization that decision-making means trading one set of problems for a different set.

The "trade-off" or "costs" of the values in the Methodist system of ministerial placement include these factors: (1) there are comparatively severe limitations on the upward vocational mobility of pastors under 40 years of age (for example, in 1958 only 10.2 percent of all Methodist district superintendents were under 45; in 1970 this figure was 12.6 percent [10]); and (2) the welfare of the minister is frequently given priority over the welfare of the congregation when appointments are made. Or, to make the same point from another perspective, in many of the judicatories of the denominations in which congregations "call" their own pastors, a decrease in mobility in general and a very sharp decrease in the vocational opportunities open to ministers aged 50 and above is traded for a greater range of vocational opportunities for younger ministers and for a pattern of more frequently (but not always!) placing the needs of the congregations above the welfare of the ministers.

There is no question but that the characteristics, size, inertia, conservatism, and instinct for institutional self-preservation of the denominations do obstruct actions that many individual church members believe to be highly desirable. What is the alternative? If the disadvantages of denominationalism are eliminated, what will replace the advantages that will disappear with them?

Though it is now ancient history, a good example of this can be found in the efforts during the 1960s to organically unite several of the larger Protestant denominations under the umbrella of the Consultation on Church Union (COCU). A strong case can be developed for the argument that the largest single barrier to Methodist participation in such a union was the comparatively large differences in the funding of the various denominational pension funds. While it was rarely mentioned, this discrepancy probably was an insurmountable barrier for the Methodists. In order for the several denominations to become one, *and* for ministers to be completely free to move across former denominational barriers, "the pension problem" would have had to be solved.

Basically the problem is relatively simple to explain. In the Christian Church (Disciples of Christ) and The United Presbyterian Church in the U. S. A. the denominational pension program is almost fully funded. In The United Methodist Church, by contrast, the *total* ministerial pension system (which is really a collection of subsystems) on January 1, 1972, had total liabilities of $548,950,000, of which $439,290,000 was *not* funded. This means that 20 percent was funded. Now what would happen when a Methodist minister traded pulpits in the new united denomination with a pastor from what had been a Presbyterian church? Would this unfunded liability travel with the former Methodist minister and be picked up by the former Presbyterian church? Or would it remain with the former Methodist congregation, which would carry that financial liability and also pay the full cost of continuing the funded pension of its new, former Presbyterian minister? Or would that unfunded pension liability be assumed by all the congregations in the new united church along with the much smaller unfunded liabilities of the other denominations? An easy way—on paper —to resolve this problem would have been for The United Methodist Church to fully fund its pension system before church union was consummated. For the annual conference with 200,000 members and an *average unfunded pension liability* this would have meant a capital funds drive to raise $9 million for the pension fund in order to enter the new united church on an equal basis with the United Presbyterians and the Christian Church (Disciples of Christ). There are some annual conferences where it would have been difficult to have a motion to that effect adopted and implemented.

The natural response of action-oriented church members to such explanations is often "That's our problem! Those cumbersome denominational boards are always throwing housekeeping concerns in the path of the people who are most concerned about the mission of the church and believe they are called to be obedient to God's will."

While such a response may have cathartic or therapeutic values, it contributes little in a creative sense to the decision-making process. A more productive approach would be to begin to identify alternative solutions to "the pension problem," or to suggest "trade-offs" whereby all parties to the consultation negotiations would trade off certain pension benefits in order to expedite union.

The Question of Scale

The presence of institutions similar to what are now referred to as "denominations" is essential in order for the individual worshiping congregations to respond in faithfulness and obedience to the call of the Lord. Whether they should be relatively small and comparatively simple institutional structures or large and complex organizations is another issue. In general, the more responsive the national denominational structure is to the needs of individuals, congregations, and regional judicatories, the more complex it will be. This fact is illustrated by the present structure of The United Methodist Church and the structure of The United Presbyterian Church before the shift to regional synods.

One of the trade-offs for the values present in a large and complex denominational structure is a loss of intimacy and an increase in the feeling that "the organization is running things rather than having people control the organization." This was revealed very clearly by two recent denominational mergers, each involving one large and one comparatively small denomination.

In 1958 the United Presbyterian Church of North America, with 258,000 members, united with the 2.8-million-member

77

Presbyterian Church in the U.S.A. Ten years later the merger of the 750,000-member Evangelical United Brethren Church and the 10.2-million-member Methodist Church was completed. In both cases leaders in the smaller denomination felt they were being "swallowed up" by the institutionally complex, theologically more liberal, bureaucratically more impersonal, and numerically much larger denomination. In both cases a great effort was made to "take care of" individual ministers in the smaller denomination. Many moved into leadership positions that carried greater responsibilities, more status, and a larger salary than would have been available to them if they had not united with a larger denomination. The trade-off was to watch with sorrow as many of the beloved churches, institutions, associations, publications, and special projects of the smaller denomination were merged, dissolved, abandoned, sold, neglected, or radically altered.

While the costs and benefits of scale are illustrated most vividly by the union of a large denomination with a smaller one, they are always present. In the Evangelical Mennonite Brethren Conference, for example, 18 percent (7 out of 37) of the ordained clergy serve on the Executive Committee of the denomination. By contrast, in the Lutheran Church in America only one-fourth of one percent of the ordained clergy serve on the national Executive Committee of the denomination.

In general the complexity of the organization increases with size and/or with the sensitivity and responses to human need. This increase in scale almost automatically produces an increase in the degree of probable alienation of the individual member from the organization. One result is that the proportion of inactive members tends to be smaller in the 20-member congregation than in the 200-member congregation, and the proportion in the 200-member parish tends to be lower than it is in the 2,000-member congregation. A second result of this factor is that when two 40-member congregations unite the result tends to be a congregation of 70 to 80 members, while the merger of two 700-member congregations tends to produce a new congregation which, a few years after the merger has been completed, has 700 to 1,000 members. A third result is summarized in the frequently heard comment from a proponent of a denominational union speaking from the perspective of five years after the consummation of the merger: "If I had known what the cost was going to be, I believe I would have voted against the merger proposal."

To some this may appear to represent a gloomy view of institutional pressures on the decision-making processes of the churches. The intent is to convey neither cheer nor gloom, but rather to emphasize the importance of institutional factors in decision-making.

What Are the Choices?

It is not unusual to hear a leader in a congregation comment very critically about the discrepancy between the biblical images of the church and the practices of denominational agencies. Similar comments are often heard about the gap between the Protestant emphasis on the priesthood of all believers and the clergy's domination of the denominational machinery. When the allocation of financial resources is being discussed, it is not uncommon for someone to point to the incompatibility between the pleas for congregational initiative and the repressive practices of denominational agencies and leaders.

The discrepancy between religious theory and denominational practice was what inspired Paul Harrison's classic study of the influence of institutional pressures in the American Baptist Convention.[11] Harrison pointed out, and later studies by Val Clear, Gibson Winter, and others[12] confirmed the point, that religious organizations develop, grow, and function similarly to other institutions and with little regard to, or influence by, ecclesiology. Pragmatic considerations win out over theological factors. That the dream of greater institutional efficiency in the future can offset the ethnic, nationality, and language differences of the past was demonstrated by the union of three Lutheran bodies in 1960 which produced The American Lutheran Church, and another one two years later which united four other Lutheran denominations to form the Lutheran Church in America.

The choice for the church member in contemporary America is not between no institutionalized church bureaucracy and denominationalism. It is not a choice between left and right or black and white. The choices today have been reduced to a range of grays in the middle of the spectrum of institutionalism.

One choice is on size, a choice that might be illustrated by the Moravian Church in America, with 149 churches, 217 ordained clergy, and 57,000 baptized members, a short distance from one end of this spectrum reflecting size; the Presbyterian Church in Canada, with 1,069 congregations, 866 ordained clergy, and 183,000 members, near the center of this spectrum; the Southern Baptist Convention, with 35,000 congregations and 12 million members near the other end of the spectrum; and the Roman Catholic Church with 23,800 parishes, 48 million members, and nearly 58,000 ordained clergy, at the extreme end of this spectrum of size. There are approximately forty denominations in the United States and Canada which are scattered between the Presbyterian Church in Canada and the Southern Baptists on this spectrum of the size of religious denominations. These are the religious bodies with between 185,000 and 12 million members. There are another forty religious bodies in the United States and Canada scattered along this size spectrum between the Moravian Church and the Presbyterian Church in Canada. There are a couple of hundred other small religious bodies not as large as the Moravian Church which should not be ignored completely, but 95 percent of all people identifying themselves as church members in the United States and Canada have selected a congregation in a religious body with at least 50,000 members. Thus the practical range of choice on size appears to range between a denomination the size of the Moravian Church in America and a very large one such as the Roman Catholic Church, the

Southern Baptist Church, or The United Methodist Church. A second choice is in the expression of institutionalism. The six basic choices are: (1) a denomination dominated by pastors, such as The Lutheran Church–Missouri Synod; (2) a denomination in which every level of church government is "autonomous," such as the Disciples of Christ or the United Church of Christ, but which includes very strong centralist tendencies; (3) a denomination which is really a federation of regional administrative units, such as the Mennonite Church; (4) a highly centralized denomination which is a congregation of congregations (but with growing tensions over this) such as The American Lutheran Church; (5) a denomination which is a federation of regional judicatories in tension with a very loose coalition of national agencies, such as The United Methodist Church; or (6) a denomination which is tied together by a shared heritage, personal relationships, and mutual trust rather than institutional relationships, such as the Cumberland Presbyterian Church.

Many of those who are dissatisfied with the pressures of institutionalism and who are not inspired by this range of choices have been seeking another alternative. Dissatisfaction with the institutional status quo reached such a level during the middle and late 1960s that is has produced an unprecedented degree of interest in tinkering with the ecclesiastical machinery.

4 Tinkering with the Machinery

The decade spanning the years from 1965 to 1974 may be described as that period in American church history when interest in several of the long-established "mainline" denominations gradually shifted from evangelism, social action, and outreach to an unprecedented concern with overhauling the ecclesiastical machinery. This is not to suggest that tinkering with the machinery occupied the attention of all American Christians. Concurrently with the emphasis on improving the organizational structure of Presbyterian, Mennonite, Lutheran, Roman Catholic, Methodist, and other denominational and inter-church organizations, two other sets of events were taking place. One was the vigorous growth of many so-called "evangelical" and independent churches. The other was the far more rapid spread of the Charismatic Renewal Movement.[1]

For many of the leaders in the churches, however, the focus in decision-making was on "restructure." Among the earliest in this period was the restructuring of the Christian Church (Disciples of Christ) which was officially adopted in 1967 to be effective in 1968 and, in one sense, "completed" in October, 1973, when one of the chief architects of that effort, Kenneth L. Teegarden, was elected as general minister and president to succeed A. Dale Fiers. In this restructure the Christian Church (Disciples of Christ) moved from a loose federation of congregations and semi-autonomous regional and national societies and boards to become a three-tier denomination with each layer (congregations, regional units, and international agencies) retaining a very high degree of autonomy.

Several other denominations began the process of restructure in the late 1960s and officially adopted a new plan in 1971 or, more often, in 1972. The Mennonite Church, which had been a federation of congregations with the power concentrated in twenty districts rather than in national agencies, started the

82

process of review in 1965 and adopted the results of this study in 1971.

In several cases the reorganization was largely a result of financial pressures. Two examples of this are the reorganization of the National Council of Churches of Christ in the U.S.A. (NCC) in 1972, and the development of an interdistrict organization in the Unitarian Universalist Association in 1968. In a somewhat similar manner the restructuring of the Cumberland Presbyterian Church in 1971 was motivated by the need to develop a better system for making decisions on the allocation of scarce resources.

In some respects this emphasis on tinkering with the machinery gained its greatest visibility in metropolitan, state, and national councils of churches. In sereral cases restructure moved to the top of the agenda as the number one priority in the allocation of staff and board time. Frequently this emphasis on reorganization was both the product and the source of a growing apathy toward the conciliar movement.

In considering the many attempts to restructure the ecclesiastical machinery, it may be helpful to review the major trends, to look at what happened, and to discuss briefly a few of the major issues that floated to the top in the process.

General Trends

While not every one of these trends appeared in every one of the efforts at restructure, certain patterns recurred with such frequency that they can be defined as trends.

1. The most significant single trend was the identification of the worshiping congregation as the primary client of the denominational structures. The most obvious dimension of this trend was the replacement of a series of functional departments (evangelism, stewardship, etc.) with a new department concerned with servicing the congregations. In The American Lutheran Church, for example, several of these functional departments were united in the new Division for Life and Mission in the Congregation. In the Lutheran Church in America the

parallel organization is the Division of Parish Services. In the Mennonite Church it is the Board of Congregational Ministries, and in The United Methodist Church it is the Board of Discipleship. The parallel agency in the Anglican Church in Canada is the Division of Parish and Diocesan Services.

Instead of emphasizing denominational interest in the traditional functional categories of worship, evangelism, lay activities, education, stewardship, etc., the typical new structure focuses attention on the worshiping congregation as a unit.

This should not be misinterpreted as suggesting that the primary emphasis in the restructured regional or national denominational unit is on servicing congregations. That is not true. The worshiping congregation, rather than a function such as evangelism, is seen as the primary *client*. The primary *emphasis* in the regional and national judicatories is still on the institutional health of that judicatory! The strongest institutional instinct is still self-preservation. This point can be illustrated by examining salary schedules, by reviewing which positions are abolished when funds are reduced, or by examining the priorities in the actual scheduling of staff time.

2. The most widespread, and probably the most meaningless, trend in the restructuring process was the change of names. The most highly visible of these was the change of the name of one denomination from the American Baptist Convention (a name adopted in 1950 to replace Northern Baptist Convention) to American Baptist Churches in the U.S.A.

In most of the other restructure efforts the names of several national denominational agencies were changed.

3. One of the two or three most significant trends was in the direction of regionalism. The most dramatic move in this direction was made by The United Presbyterian Church, which created large and very influential regional synods. This has greatly increased the power of the regional unit, while decreasing the power of both the presbyteries and the general assembly agencies. In making the synods the critical organizational units the United Presbyterians are developing a structure

resembling that of the Methodists, the United Church of Christ (except for Ohio), The Lutheran Church–Missouri Synod, the Moravian Church in America, the Episcopal Church, the Mennonite Church, and the Lutheran Church in America (although in the LCA the Synod is not as powerful as it was in the old United Lutheran Church in America, which was really a federation of synods. By contrast, The American Lutheran Church is a congregation of congregations with very limited authority lodged in the districts).

Another dimension of this shift toward regionalism (influenced in part by financial pressures) is the trend toward reducing the number of national staff members servicing congregations, and placing greater expectations on the regional judicatory to meet this need.

4. While there were a few notable exceptions to this pattern, the general trend was in the direction of reducing the number of major boards in the national denominational structure. The goal appears to have been five, but a few got down to four.

A typical pattern is seen in The American Lutheran Church, which established five national divisions: (1) the Division for Life and Mission in the Congregation, (2) the Division for Service and Mission in America (home missions), (3) the Division for World Mission and Inter-Church Cooperation (foreign missions), (4) the Division for Theological Education and Ministry, and (5) the Division for College and University Services.

5. A closely related trend was to separate "housekeeping" agencies from ministry agencies. Again The American Lutheran Church offers a typical pattern in its creation of three service boards—trustees, pensions, and publications.

6. One of the most perplexing problems facing the architects of restructure was how to create a national executive committee of the denomination which would have authority to make decisions between the regular sessions of the denomination's legislative body held once every two or three or four years.

In the normal institutional manner this void had often been filled in the past by the top-level staff members of the national agencies. Not everyone was happy with this system, however, and a major issue was where the power should be lodged between the meetings of the national church.

In one pattern the result has been to define very precisely and narrowly the authority of the chief executive officers of the regional judicatories when they meet together. These include the Council of Bishops in The United Methodist Church; the Council of (District) Presidents of The American Lutheran Church which also includes the general president of that denomination; and the Synod presidents of the Lutheran Church in America.

Another pattern has been to increase the authority of the chief executive officer of the denomination. Thus Robert J. Marshall, president of the Lutheran Church in America, Robert C. Campbell, general secretary of the American Baptist Churches in the U.S.A., Kenneth L. Teegarden, general minister and president of the Christian Church (Disciples of Christ), and David W. Preus, who replaced the late Kent S. Knutson as president of The American Lutheran Church, have a degree of authority that exceeds that held by any one official in such denominations as The United Methodist Church (which does not have a national chief executive officer), The United Presbyterian Church, the Presbyterian Church in the U.S., the Episcopal Church, or the Southern Baptist Convention.

A third pattern in this effort to reduce the power of the staff members of the several national agencies was to create what in effect is an "executive committee" of the denomination. Thus in The United Methodist Church, in which the General Conference normally meets only once every four years (although special sessions were held in 1966 and 1970 and there was a proposal for it to meet once every two years), widespread attention was focused on the new General Council of Ministries. The powers of this organization, which replaced the Program Council (born in 1968, died in 1972), include authority "to establish policies and make decisions governing the functions of the general boards and agencies of The United

Methodist Church, consistent with the actions of the General Conference, during the interim between its sessions." Another provision identified the membership, which would be largely from the laity and would include only six bishops, and stated that none of the officials of the new council could be a bishop.

To many people this sounded like the creation of an executive committee which could act between sessions of the General Conference; to others it appeared to be a major shift in the power structure of the denomination. The Council of Bishops asked for a ruling from the Judicial Council (the supreme court of The United Methodist Church) on the delegation of legislative power to the general Council of Ministries. They were sustained in their challenge by the Judicial Council, which declared the powers of the council to be limited to nonlegislative functions.[2]

The other challenge to this legislation concerned the specific denial of the possibility of a bishop becoming an officer of the new council. In this case the Judicial Council decided this was not "class legislation" and upheld the restriction. A dissenting opinion declared that "the underlying constitutional issue concerning the future role of the Episcopacy is of broad concern and of great importance to the Church."[3] In other words, this did symbolize a major power shift in Methodism!

7. The decreasing role of social welfare was reflected by various restructure proposals which took health, welfare, and social services, which formerly had been a separate major national board, and combined those functions with one or more boards to create one new agency. Thus in The United Methodist Church the functions of the former Board of Hospitals and Homes were absorbed into a reorganized subdivision of Global Ministries, and in The American Lutheran Church the social services functions were absorbed into a reorganized home missions division.

8. A significant trend that has taken several forms has been the practice of reducing the authority of the semi-autonomous national agencies.

The first step in this long process was to reduce the role and the power of the national Sunday School boards and the national women's organization. The Sunday School board's responsibilities have been absorbed by a denominational department of education, while the basic purpose of the women's organization in several denominations has been absorbed by the denominational board of missions. In both cases this restructuring has been followed by a reduction in the level of activity, participation, and financial income of these two lay-dominated movements.

The second step has been to bring the various single-purpose national "societies" which predate the formal organization under the denominational umbrella. This trend can be seen most clearly in the recent reorganization which produced the American Baptist Churches in the U.S.A., in the restructure of the Christian Church (Disciples of Christ), and in the union of two denominations which created the United Church of Christ.

Most recently this same trend can be seen in the efforts to relate the theological seminaries more closely to the denomination in the Episcopal Church.

9. Closely related to the reduction of the authority of the national agencies is a strong movement in the direction of "connectionalism" in the denominations with a strong congregational polity. This is also referred to as "mutuality" in The American Lutheran Church. Perhaps the clearest examples are the 1968 restructure of the Christian Church (Disciples of Christ), the recent reorganization of the American Baptists, and the various efforts to bring associations and conferences into a closer relationship in the United Church of Christ.

Another dimension of this trend toward emphasizing connectionalism was the pattern of encouraging the regional judicatories, and in some cases even congregations, to develop a structure paralleling that of the national denominational structure. Thus in some denominations a regional judicatory or a congregation is encouraged to use the same organizational structure and to employ the same nomenclature in describing its boards and committees as are used in the national headquarters. This is a radically different concept from the relationship of state and local governments to the national government which (*a*) encourages the concept that organizational form follows function and (*b*) encourages the state and local governments to be laboratories where new ideas may be tested. While some critics of this practice attempted to point out that the functions of a national denomination or a regional judicatory were radically different from those of the worshiping congregation, this argument, when it was heard, was answered with the plea that parallel structures were necessary (*a*) to improve communication, (*b*) to improve coordination, and (*c*) to help local church leaders know where to turn for help and guidance.

10. One of the most interesting trends is the relative minor changes in the denominational agencies charged with the responsibility for foreign missions. In most denominations there has been a major change in the national agencies concerned with various facets of ministry and mission in the United States, but only minor changes were made in the agencies concerned with ministry outside the United States. Does this suggest that discontent with performance rather than with structure was the strongest motivation for the recent wave of denominational reorganizations?

What's the Game?

Another way of looking at the various restructure efforts is to use the analogy of a ball game. This may be helpful in describing the extent of the changes.

The use of this sports analogy highlights a half dozen different types of changes. A restructure may change the name, but it may or may not be the same old game. The rules may be changed. There may be a change in the players. A fourth change may be in the nature of the game itself. There may be a change in the playing field. Finally, there is always the question of the tensions produced among the players when there are major changes. For example, the United Presbyterians abandoned an old and comfortable playing field in Philadelphia when they moved several games to New York. A number of players in Minneapolis, Nashville, Indianapolis, Chicago, Philadelphia, Atlanta, and New York who saw line-up changes coming out of restructure were nervous about whether they would be comfortable in the new position (several expected they might be given an unconditional release soon after the season opened). Others wondered whether they would be able to get along with the new coach.[4] These conditions increased the tension accompanying the arrival of several rookies who were certain to make the team. Several players knew their days were numbered and were reconciling themselves to the necessity of developing the skills necessary for a completely different game in another league.

The acute discomfort that always accompanies change was clearly visible at the 1972 Democratic National Convention, when there were several significant changes in the rules, the game was shifted to a different playing field from the one used in 1968 and an unprecedented number of young rookies made the team, several of the big-name players and scores of regulars from former seasons were dropped from the roster, and many of the players and fans were uncomfortable with the new manager.

If this sports analogy is followed, the restructure of the Christian Church (Disciples of Christ) can be described in these terms: It produced a radical change in the rules (among other changes the players were separated from the spectators and many spectators went home), it created a new playing field (a denomination to replace a very loose federation), but most of the old players were retained for the new game.

The American Lutheran Church reorganized the team by reducing the number of positions, changed a few rules and several names, resisted efforts to move the playing field from Minneapolis to the eighteen districts, sorrowfully replaced a beloved and youthful manager who had many of the details of implementation in his head at the time of his premature death, and added a few players on the farm (district) clubs; but it is still much the same old game with the same old players.

The Lutheran Church in America greatly increased the authority of the manager, made the coaches of the various specialty teams (national division executives) directly responsible to the manager, increased the authority of the farm clubs (synods) for those seeking it, shifted several players to new positions, and made it clear to everyone that the most important playing field is in New York, not Philadelphia or Chicago.

The "decentralization" of The United Presbyterian Church produced several major changes in the rulebook, greatly enhanced the importance of the synod playing field, caused a major shuffle of players both by position and by playing field, and caused some of the presbyteries to see themselves as minor league clubs. There were many name changes, and the United Presbyterians rank (with the Disciples of Christ and the American Baptists) as one of the three denominations whose restructuring efforts probably came closest to producing a new game.

The Presbyterian Church in the U.S. (PCUS) added a new playing field in the synods, but there remains the question of how many people want to play on it. They repeatedly voted in favor of merging (reuniting) with the Yankee league, which is nearly three times as large. The PCUS also encouraged more women to get into the game (as did several other denominations, some of which declared that the game could not start unless one-third of the players were female), changed a substantial number of players, released several veterans, watched 260 farm clubs vote to form a new "outlaw" league, renamed a few elements of the game, and changed a few rules. For the PCUS, however, it is still the same old game, a contest between the liberals and the conservatives.

The United Methodist Church restructure of 1972 changed

several names, merged a few of the clubs, moved several players from Chicago to Nashville or New York, made a few changes in the rules, brought up nineteen rookies to the active roster of bishops (twice the normal number), and changed a few managers and coaches. When the changes are compared to those made in several other denominations, however, it still appears to be the same old game with a great many of the same veteran players at key positions.

The American Baptists changed the name of the game, developed a brand new playing field, revised the rules drastically, created great unease on many of the farm clubs, and made it clear who is managing the new game. They also moved to reduce the "home field" advantage. Previously there had tended to be a disproportionately large number of delegates at the national convention from the geographical area in which the meeting was located. This obviously could influence the outcome of the vote on certain issues. In the new game all the persons elected by the election districts to attend the national meeting will have their expenses paid, regardless of distance, and this is expected to reduce the "home field" factor. The new rules eliminated much of the secrecy which had been a characteristic of the old Finance Committee. In the new game the allocation of financial resources will be done openly by a National Staff Council composed of the managers of all the teams in the entire system.

In the Mennonite Church the actions in 1971 created a new General Assembly which held its first meeting in Virginia in August, 1973. This replaces the national mission meeting and the youth convention. Thus they changed the name of the game, consolidated three playing fields into one, and provided for the influx of scores of new players, many of whom were expected to be lay persons. For the Mennonites, however, the game is really played in twenty places (conferences) which are grouped together into five leagues on a regional basis.

The reorganization of the National Council of Churches

probably drew fewer interested spectators than any other game of the period. Instead of placing authority in the hands of the manager as was the case with at least three denominations, the National Council followed the example of the Chicago Cubs of a decade ago when they gave control to a rotating group of coaches identified as a forty-four-member executive committee. Gate receipts had dropped so much in recent years that the council had to release over a third of the players. The debate here was more concerned with the sex, age, color, ethnic background, and political views of the participants than with the nature of the game itself or the outcome.

The ecclesiastical sportswriter of 1985, when he is reviewing some of these events, may conclude that for many denominations it was the same old game, while for others it was a game that was notable because of how briefly it was played before the demand for another round of changes became so great that the contest had to be interrupted again while the rules were changed, the teams were revised, and the playing field redesigned.

Issues and Problems

"If you don't like the existing national structure of the LCA, you probably won't like the one proposed by the Commission on Function and Structure."

This comment was made by a Lutheran pastor at a meeting in early 1972 at which the report of that commission of the Lutheran Church in America was being discussed. He was making a very perceptive point. Many objections to the operation of any organization cannot be overcome by restructuring that organization. Restructure can best be defined as one of the many methods used in organizations to trade in an old set of frustrating problems for a new set of problems.

The most widespread cause of objections to the decisions made by any representative political or ecclesiastical organization is not, as is often alleged, how the organization is structured, or the method of electing delegates, or the process of selecting staff, or the scheduling of meetings, or the content of the decisions. The most common reason for objection to an existing organizational structure is that the objectors feel excluded from the heart of the decision-making process. A widely publicized recent example of this which has been mentioned before was the "reform" which changed the rules for the selection of delegates to the 1972 Democratic National Convention.

One of the most widely used criteria for delegating authority to someone else is the confidence of the person delegating authority that the other person represents the "proper" point of view. Restructure of an organization can change who will be selected, but it cannot guarantee that everyone will be happy with the new system or with the points of view that are represented. Frequently the "outs" become the "ins," the "ins" become the "outs," and the disagreement continues.

Both the Democrats and several denominations resorted to the use of quotas, directly and indirectly, in an effort to resolve this issue. The results illustrate one of the central themes of this book: the use of quotas turned out not to be a problem-"solving" device, but rather to be an exchange of one set of problems for a new set of problems. One of the new problems produced by the use of quotas is the legal interpretation of the legislation guaranteeing quotas, and the operational difficulties presented by the reliance on quotas.

The union of 1968 which produced The United Methodist Church provided a quota for persons from The Evangelical United Brethren (EUB) Church. The basic rule was that the former EUB Church would have double its numerical representation throughout the new church for twelve years. When this was written into *The Discipline* of the new church it was stated that from 1968 to 1972, 13 percent of the delegates to the General Conference should be from the EUB membership and 87 percent from the former Methodist membership.

Recognizing that with the passing of the years there would

be members of the new church who had not been members of the two former denominations, the persons drafting the legislation sought to provide an openness for these new members of the new denomination. They specifically provided that for the quadrennium of 1972–76 at least 6.5 percent of the delegates to the General Conference must be former EUB Church members and 43.5 percent must be former Methodists. This continued the 87–13 ratio, but allowed an openness for delegates who had not been members of either antecedent denomination.

This raised the question: But how about the other 50 percent? Must the 87–13 ratio apply to the composition of the other 50 percent?

A majority of the Judicial Council said that of the 50 percent who were *not* newcomers to the new church, in other words for those in the remaining 50 percent who were either former EUB Church members or former Methodists, the proportions must be divided 87–13 in order to guarantee the former EUB members double representation in proportion to the representation of former Methodists. A minority of two (both former Methodists) in a separate opinion argued that the legislation could be interpreted to mean that the unassigned 50 percent could be elected without reference to any prior membership; they might all be from the former EUB Church, they might all be former Methodists, they might all be persons who had no connection with either former denomination, or they might be any mix of these three groups. In other words, these two men contended that the first 50 percent of the delegates must be elected on the basis of denominational heritage to guarantee the double representation of the former EUB Church, but that the second 50 percent could be elected without reference to denominational heritage.

A dissenting opinion (by a former EUB Church member on the Judicial Council) argued that the intent of the quota provision was not to guarantee an 87 percent representation to the former Methodists, but for the "single purpose" of assuring double representation for the former EUB Church in proportion to the number of former Methodists.[5]

If the argument is moved from the stage of legal interpretation to the stage of implementation, what happens? The double representation feature, according to the interpretation of the Judicial Council, provides that if sixteen persons are to be elected by one annual conference in 1975, one out of the first eight must be from the former EUB Church and the seven-to-one balance (an approximation of the 87–13 overall ratio) must be retained for the second eight. Imagine that in the actual election process in 1975 the first six persons elected are former Methodists, the seventh is a former EUB Church member, the eighth is a former Methodist, and the next four are persons who were not members of either antecedent denomination. Must one of the remaining four be a former EUB Church member? Or must all of the remaining four be persons who were not members of either of the two former denominations?

Another example of the problems created by the use of quotas can be seen in the denomination that yielded to pressures from members of the denominational women's organization and in the restructure declared that one-third of the members of one board must be lay men, one-third must be lay women, and one-third must be drawn from the clergy. In the elections that were held to fill the positions on the board, many of the women elected were not persons who had been active in, or could be considered to represent the interests of, the women's organization of the church. Should the board be expanded to include one-fourth men, one-fourth clergy, one-fourth women at large, and one-fourth women selected by the former women's organization?

Another issue brought up by the use of quotas in denominational restructuring concerns jobs. Some problems are created when jobs are filled on the basis of a quota. The situation is even more demeaning, however, to the individual who knows his job is secure in the face of a major reduction in forces because if he were dismissed the agency would be below its quota for the minority group to which he belongs.[6]

Senator George McGovern, in an April, 1973, speech to a reform group of Democrats, proposed abolition of the "guidelines" for proportional representation in the selection of delegates to the Democratic Conventions and advocated increased "participation of senior party leaders." In a series of parallel moves the next series of restructures in American Protestantism will probably trade the problems created by quotas for the problems created by disproportional representation.

While the issue of quotas has had high visibility in recent years, it is only one of many problems and issues that stand out in a review of the recent efforts to improve the ecclesiastical decision-making process by tinkering with the machinery. It may be helpful to those desiring to examine a specific denominational restructure plan to list a dozen of the more common issues, some of which were badly neglected.

1. The most common issue was the redistribution of power. This was seen in the increased use of quotas, in the shift of more power to the laity, in the struggle over the allocation of responsibilities to a reduced number of boards, in the reduction of the power of the old semi-independent societies, in the debate between vesting of authority in a chief executive officer or in a board, and in the question of how staff should be selected in nearly every other dimension of the restructure process.

2. Closely related to this was the issue of centralization. This was most clearly visible in the reorganization of the National Council of Churches. In the early discussions in 1969 and 1970 the sentiment was very strongly in favor of the decentralization of authority in harmony with what was perceived as a national trend. By the time of the Louisville meeting in January, 1971, however, the general board was ready to reverse itself and decided that decentralization would be a guarantee of ineffectiveness, and so the new structure reflects a swing toward centralization.

The old United Lutheran Church that became part of the

Lutheran Church in America was a paradox in that on the one hand it was in fact a federation of synods, but because of the personality of its president, Franklin Clark Fry, it had a very strong national office. The swing from 1962 to 1972 was toward decentralization, but the restructure of 1972 produced a strong swing back toward centralization at the national level.

There was also a strong swing toward increased centralism in the Christian Church (Disciples of Christ), among the American Baptists, and, to a much lesser degree, in The United Methodist Church. The United Presbyterian Church took the longest step away from centralization and toward regionalism. (It is somewhat ironic that while one of the arguments in the Presbyterian Church in the U.S. in favor of reunion with the United Presbyterians is that the Southern Presbyterians today are a regional church, in fact this reunion would mean merger with a denomination that has swung from a very strong national focus to a very strong regional emphasis. Some even fear that a few of the larger United Presbyterian synods will become mini-denominations.) Two of the extreme examples of decentralization in American Protestantism are to be found in the Reformed Church in America and the Moravian Church in America. In both denominations a strong history of regionalism prohibits centralist tendencies.

3. Linked to both of the above issues was the question of the power of the national meeting held every year or every two or three or four years in relationship to the power of (a) the national boards and agencies and (b) the regional judicatories. The rhetoric appears to have favored maximizing power in the national legislative convention, but the results appear to have been in the direction of reducing the effective authority of the national convention and increasing the authority of (a) the chief executive officer of the denomination, or (b) the general boards, or (c) some form of national executive committee, or (d) the regional judicatories. This was one area, however, in which there was no uniform general trend.

4. The struggle over the location of the power centers, and

the questions about the role of the national convention, raised the issue of how frequently the national denominational meeting should be held. In The United Methodist Church, for example, a proposal was submitted to the annual conferences to change from a quadrennial to a biennial schedule. (It was defeated in the 1973 meetings of the annual conferences.) In the Lutheran Church in America a proposal was prepared, to be acted on at the Baltimore convention in June, 1974, to change from the established pattern of a large (700-member) convention meeting once every two years to a smaller (250 representatives) legislative body meeting annually.

Here again the trade-off principle applies. The advantages of the larger gathering meeting less frequently include a broader participation, greater chances for inspirational events, opportunities for more people to feel a part of the larger church, more chances for firsthand reporting to the churches "back home," and a greater diversity of opinion. These benefits have a price tag which includes the dollar cost; the inability of any large group to function effectively as a legislative body when it meets only for a week or two once every two or three or four years and a large proportion of the participants are attending their first convention; the vulnerability to control by the professional bureaucrats; the increasing pace of change which makes it impossible for a group meeting only once every two or three or four years to respond to current issues; and the inability of such a large group meeting only occasionally to respond to anything except the "managed" agenda.[7]

5. One of the two major issues that was identified least clearly was the widespread discontent with the fact that the real control over program priorities has rested with the budget-makers rather than with the program people. A variety of fumbling efforts were made to deal with this issue, some of which sounded very impressive but remain to be tested. In general, it appears that the basic national trend toward designated giving by individuals, congregations, and regional judicatories means that the question of whether the control of

program priorities at the national level is in the hands of the budget-makers or the program people is not a very important issue. It is a very important issue, however, in congregations and regional judicatories. At both points the trend is toward reducing the power of the budget-makers and increasing the power of the program committees. The pace of change, however, is perhaps 1 or 2 percent a year in most places.

6. Unquestionably the most serious issue in the restructure process, and also the one that was presented with the least clarity, was the failure to distinguish clearly between reducing expenditures and cutting costs. One of the motivating factors behind all of the recent wave of restructure plans was that denominational receipts have not increased during the inflationary period that began in 1964 as fast as they did during the inflationary period of 1951–55 (see pages 145-50). The combination of this pressure and the relatively simplistic approaches to restructure required in a voluntary association in which much of the authority over the restructure proposal is in the hands of part-time volunteers meant that the focus was on reducing expenditures and improving efficiency rather than on economy, reducing costs, and improving effectiveness, which are radically different subjects.

In several respects the approach to ecclesiastical restructure in the 1965–73 period resembled the approach used in the Department of Defense in the Robert S. McNamara era. In both cases a basic assumption was that the "information-analysis-directive approach" to management of a large institution will produce improved results with reduced expenditures. Another basic assumption was that the officials in these institutions will act in the general interest (see pages 50-52 and 177-79 concerning "frame of reference"). Both assumptions neglect many aspects of the behavior of institutionalized bureaucracies functioning within the context of representative government. The behavior of the Department of Defense is an outstanding indication of the relevance of that statement, and of the inadequacy of both these two assumptions!

In the ecclesiastical restructure efforts, the models used in developing restructure proposals were, first of all, ecclesiastical models; second, sociological models (most of the literature on bureaucracy has been written by sociologists); and third, political. All three, and especially the first two, tend to neglect the relevance of the personal preferences of the professional staff members of the bureaucracy.

The use of either an ecclesiastical or a sociological model in restructure efforts meant that the focus would be on continued acceptance of inadequate organizational systems because of an overriding concern that certain types of services should continue to be supplied to the churches. It meant that the emphasis would be confined to reducing expenditures and improving the efficiency of existing systems rather than on opening up for examination the larger questions of cutting costs and improving effectiveness.

While only indirectly related to recent restructure efforts, a simple illustration of this very fundamental issue is theological education. The cost of operating theological seminaries has been rising at an average of 10 percent per year for over a decade. How should the churches respond to that problem? By increasing the amount of money available to the seminaries? By merging the smaller and "less efficient" seminaries with larger ones? By reducing the expenditures by eliminating the subsidized dormitories and the subsidized dining rooms? Or by looking at other methods of training persons for the professional ministry? The first three are the only alternatives available if an *ecclesiastical* model is used to consider the issue. If an *educational* model is used, however, it opens up consideration of the fourth alternative and opens the door to other considerations of how costs could be reduced.

Similarly, the use of an economic model of the bureaucracy in a voluntary association would have opened new doors for the persons on restructure committees considering the services provided by denominational agencies. This would have enabled them to give serious consideration to such matters as the reduction in the costs of some services, the merits of redundancy,[8] alternative methods for improving the effectiveness of the ecclesiastical bureaucracy through structural changes, and the use of incentive plans. The failure to use an economic model in examining the ecclesiastical bureaucracy, plus the naïve assumption that elimination of duplication and competition among denominational agencies will reduce costs and improve efficiency, practically guarantees that the discontent which motivated the recent round of denominational restructure efforts will be around to generate another series of restructure proposals in the late 1970s and early 1980s.[9]

7. Closely related to point 6 is the issue of whether the focus of a restructure effort should be on the various layers of the ecclesiastical structure or on the interfaces between the layers.

In the recent wave of restructure efforts the focus was more on the layers than on the interfaces. One result of this was that in some denominations the tail began to wag the dog as congregations and regional judicatories were asked to change their own organizational structure in order to relate to the national denominational agencies more effectively or to make it easier for the national agencies to promote their program in the regional judicatories and in the congregations.

8. Another area where the rhetoric greatly outdistanced the performance was on the issue of "top down" versus "bottom up" as the approach to restructure. Given the centuries of practice in the hierarchical style of denominational organization, and given the fact that most church members, both lay and clergy, have been trained to function in this organizational context, it probably was unrealistic to expect anything else.

In the next round of restructure efforts, however, it is probable that the approach will be to use the experiences and the best practices of congregations and regional judicatories as an important point of departure for proposing changes in national denominational organizations.

9. Another major difference between the recent series of

restructure plans and the next series is that probably the next round will place greater emphasis on use of an economic model of bureaucracy (see point 6 above) and be more clearly a goal-centered process. Most of the recent restructure plans appear to have been motivated more by discontent with the existing structure than by any carefully worked-out goals that could be achieved by a change.

10. Another issue that was widely and seriously discussed in the recent series of restructures was the style of leadership. Here again rhetoric exceeded performance, and in some denominations the two even went in opposite directions. The impact of recent developments in business administration (see chapter 8) had a great impact on many participants in the restructure processes, and as a result much was heard about "collegiality" and "shared leadership." The overall trend, however, with only a few major exceptions, was to strengthen the rigidity of the pyramid-shaped hierarchy.

11. Perhaps the most perplexing issue was what should be done about the informal caucuses that have emerged in several denominations in recent years.

The American Baptists moved in the direction of encouraging the formation of caucuses by the creation of "election districts." The Methodists, who have more active caucuses than any other denomination, offered various kinds of patronage to some and ignored others. The Disciples of Christ, with "the Fellowship for a Free and Responsible Church" and "the Disciples for Mission and Renewal" representing two very different points of view, have tried to keep the door open to all while at the same time defining the boundaries of the denomination. Many members of The Lutheran Church–Missouri Synod are dismayed over the politicizing of that denomination by the formation of a "conservative" caucus and the subsequent emergence of a counter group that is labeled "moderate" or "middle-of-the-road."

At this point in history it appears that the politicizing of the larger denominations has reached the point where the caucus should be recognized as a fact of life, although its impact on the decision-making processes will probably diminish before it rises again to the heights of 1970–72. One of the reasons for this prediction is that the ecclesiastical Establishment has developed a relatively high level of skill in defusing all but the most extreme caucuses by giving them at least an informal place at the decision-making table. This was one of the most significant lessons to come out of the 1972 round of denominational and interdenominational conventions.

12. Finally, the experiences of the 1965–74 decade have produced a series of generalizations about the restructure process that undoubtedly will be utilized in the next round. This point can be illustrated either by the contents of this chapter or by lifting up a few of these generalizations or guidelines:

a. The policy-makers, the clientele to be served, and the sources of financing should all be represented in any central decision-making body.

b. The consumer of services must have at least as strong a voice in any restructure process as the producers of the services (see point 6 above and pages 162-66).

c. The closer the decision-making process is to the point of implementation of the decision, the less vulnerable the operation is to the ravages of institutional blight and institutional repressiveness.

d. The place in the organizational structure at which funds are allocated will determine to a large degree the purposes for which those funds can be allocated (see pages 30-32).

e. Power must be visible to be controlled responsibly.

f. For any decision made at any point in the denominational structure, there must be at least one open, recognized, and legitimate avenue of appeal at that organizational level.

The participant in any restructure effort, new or old, will want to add to this list of generalizations, but in doing so he may find it helpful to be aware of the political and patronage dimensions of the decision-making processes, regardless of the polity or the denominational label.

5 Polity, Politics, and Patronage

Polity

Nearly all congregations in American Christendom are governed by one of two forms of church government. Congregations which are able to pay all their bills usually function under a *congregational* system of church government.[1] Congregations which require assistance from the denomination in paying their bills are involved in some *connectional* form of church government. A brief review of three basic principles in church government will help explain the similarities and differences between these two forms.

The first principle is that the only common discipline binding on all churches and all church members is an economic discipline. (See chapter 7 for details of the impact of money on decision-making.)

The second principle is that the easiest way for a congregation involved in a connectional form of church government to gain the greater freedom that is a part of the congregational polity is by raising enough money to pay all its own bills.

The third principle is that for the congregation in a denomination which ostensibly follows a connectional form of church government (Presbyterian and United Methodist are two examples), the easiest means of increasing its own congregational autonomy is by becoming more connectional in budgeting its financial receipts. In other words, the Presbyterian or United Methodist congregation which allocates half of its financial receipts to denominational causes has a greater degree of autonomy than the congregation which allocates 20 percent of its receipts to denominational causes and 40 percent to benevolent causes which are completely outside the denominational umbrella. In most cases the first of these two congregations will have greater freedom in selecting its own pastor or in moving to a new location or in undertaking a major building program or in influencing the allocation of denominational resources than will the second.

These three principles run counter to most of the rhetoric about church government, and many readers will object, "But that's not the way it is in *our* denomination!" They are partially correct. That is not the way the book of church government reads in their denomination. They are also correct in that exceptions can be cited to these general principles in every denomination. An examination of the decision-making process in operation, however, reveals a remarkably large number of times when all three principles are descriptive of what has happened. This is at least as true in the Roman Catholic parishes in the United States as it is in Lutheran or Episcopal or United Methodist circles.

Despite the differences in denominational labels and in the words in the various books of church government, the churches in the United States and Canada are moving toward a common ground where the differences in polity are overshadowed by the similarities. In addition to the general utility of the three principles stated above, there are several other similarities in polity among the various religious bodies.

First of all, there are usually *three important focal points* for decision-making within the denominational family. These are the congregation, a regional judicatory, and the national church headquarters. If there are four such focal points in the organizational structure, one of them usually ceases to be an important arena for decision-making. In The United Presbyterian Church, for example, the new structure provides for four important decision-making points—the congregation, the presbytery, the regional synod, and the general assembly and its agencies. Several proponents of the new structure contend very seriously that the power gained by the recently created regional synods was at the expense of the national agencies and that the presbyteries did not lose any power in the new process. If this turns out to be the way the new system operates, it will be a marvel to behold.

The United Church of Christ has four autonomous decision-making levels—congregation, association, conference, and national—but, except in Ohio, the three important ones are the congregation, the conference, and the national levels. Likewise The United Methodist Church has four important decision-making points—congregation, district, annual conference, and national—but it has never been successful in making both the district and the conference important points of meaningful decision-making.

Perhaps the area in which the denominations are moving closer together at the fastest pace is pastoral placement. On the one hand the appointive system used by Methodism is changing to resemble the call system used by most other denominations. The influence of the congregation (if its leaders are willing to make the effort to be influential) in pastoral placement is increasing. Likewise pastors have a far more influential voice in the process than was the case twenty or thirty years ago. In many annual conferences the method of pastoral placement is a shared decision-making process which is steered by the cabinet (bishop and district superintendents), but the control is shared and there are several points of potential veto.

On the other hand, in most of the denominations in which congregations "call" their pastor the trend is toward increasing the influence of the chief executive officer and the staff of the regional judicatory in the placement process. In many Episcopal dioceses in the United States the bishop "recommends" three or four or five names to the vestry, and they usually limit their consideration to the names on that list. Likewise in Presbyterian, United Church of Christ, Baptist, Disciples of Christ, and Lutheran circles the influence of the chief executive officer of the regional judicatory is often very strong. It is not unusal for a congregation in one of these denominations to extend a call to the number one recommendation of the regional executive.

Regardless of the polity, several denominations are moving toward a common ground in the allocation of benevolence funds by congregations. Regardless of polity, an increasing number of congregations send between 70 and 100 percent of the dollars of their total benevolence giving to denominational headquarters to be disbursed through denominational channels. The tremendous variety of causes which appeal to local churches for funds makes it imperative that these requests should receive a careful and informed evaluation. Few congregations are equipped to do this with the same skill and objectivity that are available at the denominational level. The use of the regional office of the denomination as the point at which to apportion benevolences can be justified by three considerations. It is close enough to each local congregation for the specific cause to have meaning and significance. The decision will be influential at the local church level because the regional office of the denomination is geographically and administratively close enough to the local church to involve local church representatives in the actual decision-making process. Informed and objective appraisals of most of the various appeals can be made at the regional level. Such an evaluation can draw on both the time and ability of local leaders and the resources of national denominational boards.

Another area in which the denominational decision-making processes increasingly resemble one another, without regard to polity, is in the bureaucracy of the churches. The various boards, commissions, and departments with full-time professional staff members have gained a very important and influential voice in every denomination. This is the ecclesiastical counterpart of "the managerial revolution" which occurred in business and industry some years ago and is now occurring in government. An increasing number of the questions confronting a denomination involve exceedingly complex issues and require a high degree of expertise to answer. One result is that the advice and counsel of staff members is frequently the decisive factor on any given issue.

This first becomes apparent in the decisions that are made by the legislative agencies of the denomination. Subsequently the influence of the full-time staff is reflected in the items which appear on the agenda of the denomination's legislative body. The implementers of policy become the initiators of the policies they are charged with implementing. For example, in The United Methodist Church the General Conference is the principal legislative body of the church. It meets once every four years, and very few proposals receive serious consideration, much less approval, unless the proposal either originated in one of the major national boards or has had the prior approval of one or more of these agencies. Paul Harrison points out that in the American Baptist Convention, where congregational autonomy has been a basic tenet, "the power of policy initiation and determination no longer rest with the local church, but rather with the technically experienced full-time leadership." [2]

This same pattern of an increasing reliance on full-time staff members prevails at other levels, such as conferences, synods, associations, and districts. It is generally true in the churches, as in business and government, that the larger the administrative unit, the greater the influence of the full-time "staff" members. When you regularly accept and act on the advice of another person, you transfer to him part of your decision-making power.

Historically there was a distinct difference in the degree of congregational autonomy among Protestant churches, and this difference was primarily a result of variations in polity. Today there are also differences among local churches in the degree of autonomy each possesses. Some relate to their denomination very closely; some are very independent. However, today the basis for the differences appears to be less a matter of polity and more a function of (1) the attitude of the pastor toward the denomination, (2) history and tradition, (3) the comparative affluence of the congregation, and (4) the interest that leaders in the regional judicatory have in building ties between the congregations and the denomination.

In summary, despite the many pious statements that "the polity of our denomination is drawn directly from the New Testament form of church order," it is increasingly apparent that the differences in polity are more apparent than real. The elusiveness of the New Testament form of church order,[3] combined with institutional pressures, has led most of the churches in the United States and Canada to find a common ground in church order. The differences are now mainly a reflection of such factors as size, ethnic heritage, language, self-image of the pastor, wealth, geography, and traditions.

The similarities among the denominations in how decisions are made, despite apparent differences in polity, are even more striking when we consider church politics.

Politics

When a defeated congressman is given a seat on, for example, the Federal Trade Commission or the Federal Power Commission, or when a faithful party worker is rewarded with a judicial post, righteous churchmen shrug it off and mutter, "That's politics for you!"

When a district attorney contends that the ballot box was stuffed at a local election, a few people may get excited, but most will only ask, "What else did you expect from a bunch of crooked politicians?"

When a state university parallels the course offerings of a prematurely senile English professor, someone may begin to raise an objection, but he will be reminded, "The department is only taking care of its own people."

When state legislatures refused to reapportion legislative districts, with a resulting overrepresentation of sparsely populated rural areas and the underrepresentation of heavily populated urban areas, the United States Supreme Court was warned to stay out of this "political thicket."

The common response of churchmen is to accept these as natural disorders of the body politic—and to thank God that it is possible to keep the church out of politics and to keep politics out of the church.

This is, of course, a very naïve attitude. Political considerations govern the decision-making process of the institutional expression of the church just as they do the operations of governments, corporations, universities, and other social institutions. Each of the above illustrations can be duplicated in contemporary American Protestantism.

Recently a major denomination wanted to replace the top executive in one of its major national agencies. He had been a faithful worker in the vineyard, but he was unable to fulfill the administrative responsibilities of his job. After an attempt to "kick him upstairs" to a more prestigious but less responsible post within the denomination was unsuccessful, a position was found for him in a council of churches.

In another denomination a second-echelon executive began to fail and to fall behind in his work. Since it would be eight years before he could retire, another department was established and most of the important responsibilities were shifted to the new agency. The older man was kept on in his original post and never knew that it was generally understood that his department would be eliminated as soon as he retired.

In many denominations the system of representative government is weighted heavily in favor of the small churches so that one-half of the delegates at the annual meeting may come from churches which include one-fourth or one-fifth of the members in the synod, conference, presbytery, district, or diocese. While many prominent Protestant churchmen were defending the concept of "one man one vote" in the reapportionment of state legislatures, Protestant denominations' continued the underrepresentation of the large (usually urban) congregation and the overrepresentation of the small (usually rural) churches.

Politics and patronage are important factors in the decision-making process in any social structure, and, while many churchmen will continue in vain to seek to eliminate these considerations, it may be more realistic and constructive to recognize these facts of institutionalism and seek to control them rather than be governed by them. The central thesis of this book bears repeating here. The institutional expression of the church is a legitimate order of creation, and alert Christians will recognize this fact of life. Thus, instead of fighting institutionalism, they will accept it as a given and seek to function constructively and creatively within the institutional framework.

Is it inevitable that many of the decisions made within the institutional framework of the church will be "political" decisions? If one accepts the proper definition of *political* (and does not confuse it with *partisan*) the answer must be in the affirmative.

Two social scientists have suggested that a political decision is one which includes three elements: "coordinated allocation of scarce public resources, the use of governmental machinery, and choices between public and private purposes." [4]

This can easily be translated to the framework of religious rather than governmental institutions. *In the church a political decision is one which involves the allocation of scarce resources (ministerial manpower, lay leadership, church receipts, benevolence funds, etc.) the use of ecclesiastical machinery (the session, official board, church council, annual conference, presbytery, synod, diocese, etc.), and choices between different purposes (hire more staff or put up a new educational wing, subsidize additional inner-city work or organize more new churches in suburbia, seek an assistant for the denominational executive or put more money into the local council of churches).*

Another very relevant definition is offered by an Australian political scientist who wrote, "The essence of a political situation, as opposed to one of agreement and routine is that someone is trying to do something about which there is not agreement; and is trying to use some form of government as a means and as protection. Political situations arise out of disagreement. . . . Politics, then, is about disagreement or conflict; and political activity is that which is intended to bring about or resist change, in the face of possible resistance." [5]

A few examples will illustrate the variety of political decisions confronting Protestant churchmen. Should the local church elect its best leaders as delegates to the local council of churches, or keep the best leaders for service on congregational committees and send the second- or third-best layer of laymen to the council? Should the denomination concentrate its home mission funds on social action, on cooperative work with other denominations, or on building and strengthening the denomination? Should the local church raise the pastor's salary, or repair the roof of the church? *Whenever there is disagreement on alternatives the situation becomes a political situation.*

Churchmen can better understand questions such as these and participate more effectively in developing answers to them if they will recognize that political pressures are influencing the decision-making process. Comparatively few important decisions in American Protestantism are made in an administrative vacuum where all the evidence is impartially weighed, priorities are assigned on the basis of comparative need, and resources are allocated without favor or spite.

What are the results of these political factors?

The Southern Baptist Convention, which like nearly all other Protestant communions gives a disproportionate voice and vote to the small rural churches, almost invariably elects a "conservative" pastor as Convention president.

In nearly every Protestant denomination the funds for new church development are allocated on the basis of need—but also with an awareness of the political necessity of spreading the money around throughout the different geographical areas.

Benevolence support for inner-city work is allocated on the basis of need—but also is influenced by the seniority, aggressiveness, and ability of certain denominational executives who are especially persuasive in presenting their case.

The location of the regional headquarters (synod, district, conference, etc.) is determined by such considerations as transportation facilities and center of membership of the judicatory—but also by the places of residence of the members of the committee charged with that decision, and an awareness of the necessity of placating leaders from the small churches in rural areas.

The decision on whether or not the pastor should be granted a salary increase is determined in part by the funds available, the current level of salaries for churches of that size, and the quality of the pastor's work—but also by the power and influence of the chairman of the finance committee and by the attitude of the chairman of the pastoral relations committee.

Even the most superficial examination of the decision-making processes in the churches supports the contention that politics are a reality of contemporary church life. In an outstanding book on the realities of church politics, Keith Bridston observed that church politics often operate at a lower level than secular politics and are often less honest.[6] Bridston was one of the leaders in getting The American Lutheran Church to shift toward a more open political process in the election of a chief executive officer for the denomination. He also urged that a clear distinction should be made between the persons who hold political office in the denomination and those who are bureaucratic functionaries.[7] If it could be accomplished, this would probably raise the quality of ecclesiastical politics.

The politics of expediency can be found as frequently in the churches as in government or business, but perhaps less visibly. The participants may agree that a situation is not ideal, but it is "the best we can do under the circumstances." In the early part of this century Wayne Wheeler and the Anti-Saloon League would often support a candidate who was only partially acceptable on the temperance issue because that candidate could win. They would make this decision rather than back a completely acceptable candidate who could not win. A few years ago when one of the large Lutheran denominations first began to display an interest in interdenominational cooperation, a personnel committee recommended a Lutheran minister for a vacant position in an interdenominational agency. The committee did this, not because the Lutheran pastor was the outstanding candidate, but rather because they concluded, "The one sure way to get the Lutherans to cooperate in this venture is by picking a Lutheran to head the staff."

It would be possible to fill a very large book very quickly with examples of the political nature of the decision-making process in the churches. In the recent reorganization of the Presbyterian Church in the U.S., for example, the proposed synod of Alabama and Mississippi was enlarged in 1972 to include Tennessee and Kentucky. Why? Because it was deemed wise to have a very large synod in the Middle South? Or because this was one means of diluting the votes of the large bloc of conservatives in Mississippi?

In 1964 the annual conferences in the North Central Jurisdiction of The Methodist Church absorbed the Negro congregations in the Midwest which had been a part of the all-black Central Jurisdiction. In the resulting series of conference mergers, every district had a district superintendent, but because of the reduction in the total number of districts there were three superintendents left over. How many of the extra superintendents were black? Before answering this question, remember that this happened in 1964, not in the 1970s when changes in the demand produced a serious shortage of black ministers in predominantly white denominations. The political nature of the decision-making process meant that back in 1964 all three of the surplus superintendents were black.

One of the political price tags of the union of the two denominations which created the United Church of Christ was Article 21 of the new constitution. This compromise, which declares that every level of the organizational structure is autonomous, has created severe problems for the United Church of Christ and is a major reason behind proposals for organic union with either the Presbyterians or the Methodists.

Patronage

In the Southwest Ohio Association of the United Church of Christ, a denomination which for years attracted and welcomed ministers from other denominations, it has become nearly impossible for a person to be granted ministerial standing for purposes of call unless the individual is (1) a minister with standing in another association of the UCC, or (2) a seminary student under the care of the association, or (3) black.

During the 1950s nearly half of the ministers received into "fellowship" in the Universalist Church came from other Protestant denominations. In 1972 only 6 of nearly 300 ministers from other denominations who applied were granted fellowship standing in the Unitarian Universalist Association.

These two recent examples of the response to the oversupply of ministers in American Protestantism are also examples of how patronage is a factor in the decision-making processes of the churches. Simply stated, *patronage* is a political term that suggests that the distribution of resources, such as jobs or money, is based on "taking care of our own" rather than on making impartial and objective decisions on the basis of need or competence.[8]

Patronage in the churches takes many forms. One example is the pastor of a wealthy congregation who every year spends several hours between Christmas and New Year's Day responding to requests from several of his parishioners who are in high-income brackets and want advice on which causes should be on their list of last-minute tax-deductible gifts. Another is the awarding of honorary degrees. A third is the selection of persons to take an all-expenses-paid trip to visit the mission fields on another continent. A fourth is appointment to certain influential boards and committees which usually meet in attractive resort areas. A fifth is the placement of ministers (this can be seen increasingly in the denominations using the call system of pastoral placement). A sixth is the "taking care" of an old ministerial friend who has never had a happy pastorate by adding him to the denominational staff a few years before his retirement. A seventh is the merger negotiations between two denominations which guarantee a minimum number of jobs for persons from the smaller denomination and two or three very important positions for the chief architects of union. An eighth can be found in several of the denominational re-structure plans adopted in 1971 which provided new distribution points for the dispersing of patronage.

Another dimension of the patronage system in the churches can be seen in the deference pyramid.[9] People all around the world are accustomed to think in terms of a deference pyramid, although the concept is completely counter to the Christian doctrine of man.

The deferential pyramid is reflected in the use of titles in the churches, frequently with a negative impact. (See the opening section of chapter 8 for one illustration of this.)

The impact of the deferential pyramid can be seen in the decision-making processes all across the churches, and it frequently shows up in the distribution of patronage. The illustrations are without number.

The Willow Valley Church has a potluck dinner following the close of worship on the second Sunday of every month. After the Lord's blessing has been asked, everyone waits for the minister to be the first one to go past the serving table and fill his plate. Meanwhile, the hungry and impatient seven-year-old boy being physically restrained by his embarrassed mother gets another experiential learning lesson in the definiton of the deferential pyramid.

A committee of church leaders is appointed to select a home for the new bishop. Instinctively they will be influenced as much by his "rank" as by his family needs, if not more so. The local church committee to buy a new manse for the minister will be influenced by the amount of money available— and by the "rank," as they perceive it, of their church in relation to other churches. If their congregation has 1,000 members, the manse should be a little better than that owned by the 700-member church on the other side of the freeway.

Less obvious, but far more significant, is what happens when a group of churchmen, each coming from a different point on the deference pyramid, meet to decide an important question facing their church. Does each man have an equal voice in the process? Obviously not! Each may have one vote but the "politics of deference" influence both the way the votes are cast and the weight of each vote. Three persons who come from the top of the pyramid can "outvote" seven who come from near the base of the pyramid.

While many of the political, patronage, and caste considerations do obstruct the church in the fulfillment of its mission and make it more like a social order than a religious organization, there are some constructive lessons to be learned from such a comparison.

Perhaps the most important of these is the politician's emphasis on keeping in touch with the grass roots. This can be observed in the congressman who is a member of the Tuesday–Thursday Club, spending the three days in the middle of the week in Washington and Friday through Monday back in his district. It can be seen in the city councilman who attends nearly every gathering in his ward. They do this because they want to stay in office. They also do it because they want to know what their constituents are doing, saying, thinking, and wanting. This does not mean that the politician will always seek to respond to the wants of his constituents. He may also be very conscious of their needs, and his political skill helps him to comprehend the needs as well as the wants.

There is a lesson in this for the church administrator who wants to be effective. Often he finds himself too busy to keep up his grass-roots contacts—and then wonders why his decisions do not get implemented. Many church leaders today contend that the biggest problem in the ecclesiastical bureaucracy is that the denominational executives are "out of touch" with people in the local churches. While this problem may not be as real as it is said to be, there is no question but that the decision-making process would be improved if church administrators would take the political dimension of their work more seriously.

There is also a lesson here for the minister or layman who moves from the local church into a position in the ecclesiastical hierarchy. His period of adjustment will be easier if he recognizes that there are "pork barrel" considerations involved in the allocation of denominational funds, that seniority is often as important in the denominational structure as in the United States Senate, and that one of the reasons why many church leaders return for the spring convocation at the seminary is in order to attend the informal caucus which will "decide" some of the issues on the agenda for the annual meeting of the denomination in June. He will be a wiser administrator when he learns that in his denomination the critical political tension is between the "upstate" rural churchmen and the representatives from the metropolitan churches; that some of the pressure to raise the salaries of the top denominational executives is from the second-line administrators who know they cannot get an increase unless this "ceiling" is raised; and that ecclesiastical patronage comes in many forms, including funds for pet projects, status symbols such as job titles and honorary degrees, committee assignments for friends, and trips to national or international conventions. He will be a more effective decision-maker when he discovers who has the most patronage to dispense, when he realizes that political and patronage considerations are most important in those religious organizations which have the least formal structure and the fewest formal administrative rules, and when he learns how to counter these pressures.

Gradually the leaders in American Protestantism are recognizing the need for certain safeguards on the political processes in decision-making. Sometimes the safeguards are informal and self-imposed. Sometimes they are formal and established by a governing body. Thus a Methodist bishop may voluntarily ask for an advisory vote by his pastors before selecting a new district superintendent. And an association in the United Church of Christ may limit the power of the official in charge of ministerial placement by adopting a rule that a list of all vacant pulpits must be published and that every minister has the right to have his name referred to the pulpit committee of any vacant church if he requests it.

It is possible to overestimate the influence of politics and patronage when discussing the way decisions are made in American Protestantism. It is also possible, and much more probable in a pietistic climate, to underrate the influence of these considerations. In general, it appears that it is in such denominations as The Lutheran Church Missouri Synod, the Southern Baptist Convention, and the Southern Presbyterian Church, where the pious objections to "church politics" are heard most frequently, that "political" considerations are most influential in the decision-making processes of both the denomination and the churches.

Elections

In October, 1970, forty-six-year-old Dr. Kent S. Knutson, the youngest of the ten candidates nominated, was elected on the fourth ballot as president of The American Lutheran Church (ALC). A number of the delegates to that biennial convention of the ALC contend that one of the most important considerations, some argue it was the critical factor, in Knutson's election was that the election procedures allowed all ten nominees to speak to the delegates before the critical balloting began. Instead of being seen by the delegates of this denomination, which is rooted in the rich agricultural belt of the Midwest, as a scholarly seminary professor, he immediately became identified as "one of us" when he began his remarks by describing himself as a farm boy from Iowa. While his term was limited to only two years by his untimely death, Knutson was the beneficiary of the first open political campaign in the denomination's history. If none of the nominees had been permitted to address the convention until one or two ballots had narrowed the list to two or three candidates, some delegates contend, it is highly unlikely that Knutson would have been elected.

One of the clearest examples of the political nature of ecclesiastical elections can be found in the efforts to select a successor to W. A. Visser 't Hooft as general secretary of the World Council of Churches (WCC). In 1961 Visser 't Hooft announced that he planned to retire when he reached the age of sixty-five in 1965. In the fall of 1963 the WCC Executive Committee recommended to the larger Central Committee that a special nominating committee should be established which would be representative of all interests and have the responsibility of recommending a successor. This was rejected by the Central Committee, which returned the responsibility to the smaller Executive Committee and asked it to nominate the successor to Visser 't Hooft. In July, 1964, the Executive Committee announced that it had asked Visser 't Hooft to remain in office until 1966 and was recommending Patrick C. Rodger, a Scottish Episcopal priest, as his successor. In January, 1965, the Central Committee met in Nigeria and, for all practical purposes, rejected the nomination of Rodger. To many observers it appeared that the issue was not Mr. Rodger's competence, but rather a power struggle over who was going to run the World Council. A strong leader such as Visser 't Hooft? A coalition of staff members and the Executive Committee? The staff? The chairman of the Executive Committee? Or should the network of institutionalized divisions run themselves? Or should the Central Committee be the real repository of authority in the World Council? The anticlimax to this power struggle, which in a normal and predictable manner was described as a dispute over procedures, was the election in early 1966 of Eugene Carson Blake as Visser 't Hooft's successor.

When the Christian Church (Disciples of Christ) had to select a successor to the retiring A. Dale Fiers as general minister and president of the denomination, the critical decision was made by a screening committee, comprised of members from the Administrative Committee of the General Board, which considered over eighty persons, narrowed the list to two, and after several ballots nominated Dr. Kenneth L. Teegarden, the regional minister of Texas. Teegarden was selected, rather than one of the executives from the national staff, at least in part because he had both experience as a regional minister (and thus could be expected to understand the regional perspective) and also national staff experience in designing the restructure plan for the Disciples which went into effect in 1968. His nomination, like that of Patrick Rodger, also had to clear a series of hurdles, but unlike the World Council of Churches, the Disciples did not use Teegarden's nomination as the focal point for a major power struggle and he was officially elected without difficulty in October, 1973.

While the procedures used for the election of bishops in Methodism appear to deny the presence of political considerations, the facts suggest otherwise. On only five occasions before the merger with the Evangelical United Brethren did Methodists elect two men to the episcopacy from the same annual conference in the same year, the three most recent occasions being in 1944 in the Southcentral Jurisdiction, in 1948 in the Western Jurisdiction, and in 1960 in the Central Jurisdiction.[10] Translated into political terms this means that the patronage is to be passed around and not monopolized by any one conference.

Other examples of political patronage considerations in Methodism include the recently adopted provision that a newly elected bishop cannot be assigned to the area in which he was serving at the time of election;[11] the "custom" that the minister who is the last to withdraw to break a deadlock and thus hasten conclusion of the election process at one jurisdictional conference becomes the favorite for early election four years later; and the "custom" of electing as bishops only ministers who are members of the annual conferences within that jurisdiction in which the election is held. (The first of the best-known exceptions to this custom was L. H. King, who was a member of the Northeastern Jurisdiction when elected by the Central Jurisdiction in 1940. The second exception was Gerald H. Kennedy, who led on the first ballot of the South Central Jurisdiction in late June, 1944, but as a "Yankee" from Nebraska could not pick up enough "Southern" votes and withdrew after the twenty-seventh ballot. Two weeks later Kennedy was elected on the thirteenth ballot in the Western Jurisdiction.)[12]

The basic trend in American churches is toward opening up the election processes. The arguments for this include the contention that anything done *sub rosa* is more vulnerable both to an abuse of power and to suspicions of the abuse of power, actual and potential. The most highly visible recent illustration of this trend has been the last two elections for synod president of The Lutheran Church–Missouri Synod. In one of the most highly politicized elections in modern American church history, a highly articulate and aggressive conservative, Dr. J. A. O. Preus, was elected at the 1969 convention in Denver. An even more vigorous campaign was waged for the three years preceding the July, 1973, convention in New Orleans at which Dr. Preus was reelected.

This is not a uniform trend, however. Only a few months before Preus's reelection, two theological seminaries of another denomination selected new presidents. In the older of the two schools none of the faculty (with the exception of the man elected), students, or alumni knew the identity of the new president until after the trustees had announced the results of the formal election. Many of those closest to the school, including several of the new president's close friends and fellow faculty members, were completely surprised by the choice.

In the younger seminary a completely open process was used with very high involvement of students, faculty, staff, alumni, and trustees. In this seminary even the casual visitors to the campus knew the identity of the new president before the formal announcement came from the trustees.

The election processes in the church illustrate again one of the central themes of this book: there are few perfect alternatives in this world. Usually the process of making a choice means trading one set of problems for a different set.

Is the best system the "Roman ballot" in which the first ballot becomes the nominating ballot? Many church members support this system on the grounds that it minimizes the advantages of advance "campaigning" for office, provides the greatest opportunity for the Holy Spirit to guide the thoughts of electors, and gives every possible candidate an equal chance. Opponents contend that since it eliminates the opportunity to prepare information on each candidate and give this to the voters before the election process begins, the net effect is to cause some ministers and many laymen to vote from a base of ignorance, since they may know little or nothing about several of the persons named on this first ballot.[13]

Or is the best system to nominate two candidates, give both wide exposure to the electorate—and thus embarrass the loser? This often produces a more meaningful choice to the persons casting the votes, but the trade-off is that some highly qualified potential candidates will not allow their names to be submitted if this is to be the process. Some are not interested in being embarrassed by losing. Others are not interested in the possible interference with their present career if they become an identified candidate, but fail to be elected.

Another alternative is to have a nominating committee screen potential candidates and nominate one. This means either (a) transferring the actual power of selection to the nominating committee or (b) opening the door to the possibility of rejecting the committee's nominee in favor of someone nominated from the floor and thus (1) embarrassing the nominee and possibly jeopardizing his present position and/or (2) making it much more difficult to secure volunteers to serve on the nominating committee for the next election.

A third alternative is to use the "ecclesiastical ballot" throughout the entire process. This is based on the premise that the Holy Spirit will guide the hand of the person writing a name on a blank sheet of paper. New names may be placed "in nomination" by any elector on any ballot at any stage of the process. Thus a "dark horse" may be named first on the tenth ballot and elected on the twelfth to break a deadlock. Judging the merits of this alternative reflects the frame of reference of the person analyzing the process. Those who take the New Testament literally and believe in the presence of demonic forces, and those who accept the doctrine of original sin and believe that man is a sinner, will naturally have great difficulty in defending the use of the ecclesiastical ballot. Those who believe that secret political caucuses are good, who favor politicizing the election processes in the churches, and who are afraid of delegating authority to nominating committees, will tend to support the ecclesiastical ballot.

Perhaps the fundamental division over the use of an open political process in ecclesiastical elections is in regard to the power of the Holy Spirit. Some church leaders argue that an open but structured political process opens the door wider to the power of the Holy Spirit than does the ecclesiastical ballot.

The historic, but not consistently uniform, tradition of the Christian churches has been that the concept of a "call" to Christian service is violated whenever a person offers himself as a candidate for a position in the church, or even when he expresses a willingness to serve if elected. An excellent statement of this position was expressed by Dr. Oswald C. J. Hoffmann when he refused to sign a statement that he would serve if elected president of The Lutheran Church–Missouri Synod. A few months before the New Orleans convention he said, "I cannot express at this time a willingness to serve if elected, since I believe that does violence to the call I now have as speaker on the Lutheran Hour."

The long-term general trend in society in general and in the churches in particular is against the process of "unstructured decision-making" in the selection of church leaders. This can be seen in the increasing proportion of congregations that use official nominating committees to select lay leadership, in the growing number of regional judicatories in which the chief executive office "recommends" candidates to pulpit committees, and in the rapidly rising number of conferences in Methodism in which the pastor and the leaders of the congregation are structurally required to be meaningfully involved in the appointive process. (In reflecting on this trend an elderly Methodist bishop commented, "It used to be that appointments were made by the Lord and me. Now they're made by the devil and the district superintendents." A younger colleague responded, "That's no longer true. Now the appointive process is structured to involve the district superintendent, the pastor, the pastor-parish relations committee of the congregation, the pastor's wife, the number and age of his children, and occasionally even his dog.")

One of the most famous recent tests of "unstructured decision-making" in American society came in July, 1972, when George McGovern, his inner staff of some half dozen advisers, an outer ring of a dozen or more individuals, plus a miscellaneous assortment of six or eight other individuals, sat down in the Doral Hotel in Miami Beach to select a vice-presidential candidate, and chose Senator Thomas Eagleton.

When "unstructured decision-making" is defined as making everyone equal by the fact that no one person has an advantage over the rest of the group through having done any homework, a probable result is disaster. (The structured non-participatory method of selecting a vice-presidential candidate used by the Republicans in 1972 is not an attractive alternative.)

There may be a moral in that episode, both for those who believe that God is present in history and speaks in stange and mysterious ways and also for those who believe that any open acknowledgment of the existence of political considerations in the decision-making processes of the churches reflects a devilish attempt to inhibit the work of the Holy Spirit.

6 Interchurch Cooperation

The lack of money is the root of all unity.
                    Author unknown but appreciated

"It seems to me the time has come for these congregations to get together in one way or another," urged the pastor of an all-white congregation in a racially changing neighborhood. He was sitting around a table in the basement at Calvary Church with eleven other people—four ministers and eight laypersons. It was the first meeting of a task force composed of the pastor and two lay representatives from each of four all-white congregations in the Oakland community of a large midwestern city. The neighborhood had been developed in the years following World War I, and most of the houses had been built as either one- or two-family structures in the 1920s.

"I agree!" added a thirty-four-year-old layman from Trinity Church. "Our membership has dropped by over half in five years, and our receipts are down by a third. We can't go on much longer without running out of both people and money."

" I can't speak for all of our people, of course," commented a laywoman from Fourth Church, "but I believe our people are much more open to the idea of cooperation today than we were seven years ago when that other proposal for a cooperative ministry was being kicked around."

"Let's face it, friends," suggested the pastor from St. Mark's; "blacks already constitute a fifth of the population in Oakland, and the elementary school is close to 50 percent black. I doubt if any of us have more than a third of our members who live in this community. If our churches have a future it has to be in ministering to the people who will live here during the next decade. Either we cooperate or we die."

"I'll support that," declared another layman. "I think we ought to form some kind of cooperative parish out of these four churches. Maybe if we work together we can stabilize this neighborhood. If we could keep it three-quarters white and one-fourth black, I believe a lot of people would like to live here."

卍

That same week, a group of thirty-eight people, most of them over fifty years of age, met in a white frame rural church in Nebraska. They came from twenty-two different congregations, five denominations, and three counties. The discussion was being led by five denominational staff members, one from each denomination represented at the meeting.

"The question we're meeting to discuss this evening," said one of them, "is whether any of the churches represented here want to become involved in developing a larger parish. Not one church represented here has its own full-time pastor, and right now five of you are without a minister. This county reached its peak population in 1910, and the number of residents has been declining ever since. Each one of you, like many other churches in the country, is being squeezed by the continued rise in ministerial salaries and a leveling-off or decrease in income. No one is going to be forced to enter into any arrangement to which they are opposed. This is being proposed simply as one approach to a common problem."

卍

" There's no way we can raise enough money to put a full-time minister from our denomination on every college and university campus in this state," declared one person at a meeting of the denominational board concerned with campus ministries.

"Not only that, but even if we had the money, I don't believe we could find that many ministers with the skill and the interest in being a campus pastor. I don't think we have any alternative but to join this proposed ecumenical cluster. If I understand it correctly, there will be six or eight denominations sharing the responsibility for a campus ministry at every university in the state. I think we should join it."

🕎

"We only have two months left," commented one of the members of the committee charged with planning the program for the annual meeting of the state council of churches. "As I looked over the list of suggestions we have received, I believe the theme should be Christian witness. Sometime Christians in this state are going to have to stand up and be counted on these issues. Maybe this is the time and place."

Three hours later the committee had developed a list of four statements to be presented to the annual meeting. The first declared that since many studies have proved that alcoholism is the most serious drug problem in the nation, the state legislature should *either* outlaw the sale, possession, and transport of both alcohol and marijuana *or* remove the restrictions on the sale and use of marijuana. The second called on the Congress and the President of the United States to grant amnesty to all Americans in Canada who are there because of the Vietnam conflict and the draft. The third called on the state to enforce to the letter all restrictions on pollution of the air by industrial firms. The fourth called on the state legislature to remove the exemption from the general property tax for all hospitals, public and private, that refused to permit doctors to perform abortions in them.

"That's quite a list," sighed a pastor on the committee. "If I presented that list to my church council tonight I probably would have to start looking for a new job tomorrow."

🕎

"Someone has to take a stand on this issue, and it seems to me that if it's to be an effective stand it has to be by an organization that represents a lot of churches, not just one sect or denomination," declared one church leader who was opposed to the idea of granting tax credits to parents of non-public school pupils.

"I agree," came the response from his friend, "and I believe the National Council of Churches should do it."

Some time later the National Council of Churches filed a strong statement with the House Ways and Means Committee. The statement vigorously opposed the tax credit proposal and asked, "If Roman Catholics are not exerting themselves any more sacrificially than $30 or $40 per year per capita to keep their schools going, why should the rest of society make up the difference?"

Duds and Bombs

The five illustrations above have one common thread. Together they illustrate the most significant common policy underlying the decision-making process in the arena of interchurch cooperation. That policy is illustrated by these five incidents and can be stated in eight words: Hand the interchurch agency the duds and bombs.

When translated this policy says, "Let's have the interchurch agency focus on two types of concerns. One is the 'duds,' the things we aren't able to carry out effectively on a unilateral basis as congregations or denominations. The other is the 'bombs,' the projects which are too volatile or too explosive to be handled unilaterally."

A review of the five incidents described at the beginning of this chapter includes among the "duds" the effort by white congregations to respond effectively to and minister to blacks moving into a previously all-white neighborhood, the churches in a rural county which has been decreasing in population for seventy-five years and is now clearly overchurched, and the development of a denominationally oriented campus ministry with a sound financial base. In each instance no one congregation or denomination feels sufficiently competent and confident to undertake a unilateral approach to this question.

The "bombs" include the response of all-white congregations to a racially changing neighborhood, a ministry to the "radical" students on the university campus, drugs, amnesty, abortion, strict air pollution control, and opposition to public aid to Catholic schools in an era when many churches are attempting to foster Roman Catholic–Protestant relationships.

The tendency of congregations and denominations to implement unilaterally ideas which have the promise of being "winners," and of turning over to an interchurch agency those which appear to be probable "losers," is one of the most facinating dimensions of the decision-making processes in the churches today. Equally fascinating is the tendency of the leaders in the interchurch agencies to grasp eagerly for the bombs or losers and to ignore potential winners. Perhaps the generalization that fits this last statement is that there is no law against institutional suicide.

Turning Back the Clock

Another characteristic of the decision-making process in interchurch agencies is that cooperative efforts tend to attract a disproportionately large number of two types of individuals. The larger group is composed of those who have a vision of what could be in the future, but feel that this vision is beyond the grasp of either congregations or denominations and turn to an interchurch agency as a vehicle for translating that vision into reality.

The smaller group is composed of those persons who want to turn the clock back to the day before yesterday. They may be attempting to recapture the past, or they may be turning toward yesterday to escape the challenge of contemporary reality. Among the most common examples of the turn-the-clock-back syndrome are cooperative ministries in racially changing neighborhoods which enable people to focus attention on tending the machinery of interchurch cooperation instead of facing the facts of black-white relationships; forming larger parishes in some (not all!) rural communities instead of facing the fact that the county is seriously overchurched;

131

rubbing raw the almost healed-over sores of Protestant–Roman Catholic relationships; and developing a ministry to youth that will make young people want to grow up to be carbon copies of the contemporary fifty-year-old person.

Another Approach

During the 1960s and 1970s many efforts at interchurch cooperation appeared to be motivated, at least in part, by such forces as frustration, nostalgia, economy, and irresponsibility.

A more fruitful and, perhaps, also a more creative approach would be to think of all the functions, tasks, and responsibilities of congregations and denominations as being scattered along a spectrum. At the left end of this spectrum are clustered those tasks and functions which can be accomplished most effectively by a unilateral action. At the right end are clustered those which can be accomplished either (*a*) only, or (*b*) most effectively, by a cooperative approach. Scattered along the spectrum are those which do not fit comfortably at either end. This pragmatic, institutionally based, and task-oriented model is in contrast to the more widely used faith-and-order model, and is offered on the assumption that the call to the churches to ministry is as legitimate as the call to model-building.

At the left end of the spectrum are clustered four or five tasks of congregations which appear to be the ones that can be carried out most effectively on a unilateral basis. These include regularly scheduled occasions for people to gather for corporate worship, the preaching of the word, and the administration of the sacraments; Sunday School, but not necessarily all other forms of Christian education; care of the meeting place which is used for building-centered program and ministry; evangelism and the assimilation of newcomers into the fellowship of the called-out community; and, sometimes, the functioning of the women's auxiliary in the church.

At the other extreme, at the right-hand end of the spectrum, are ministries on issues, and specialized ministries which require large institutionalized operations (camps, theological seminaries, publishing houses, pension systems, housing for the elderly, hospitals, homes for orphans or for emotionally disturbed children, and some types of lay training programs). These can be accomplished most effectively on a cooperative basis, sometimes *intra*denominationally and sometimes *inter*denominationally.

At about the center of the spectrum is the vacation church school. In some situations and on some occasions it can be most effectively carried out unilaterally by one congregation, and on other occasions it can be most effectively carried out cooperatively.

About halfway between the left end and the middle is Christian education. In general, most ventures in Christian education can be most effectively implemented unilaterally, but there are so many exceptions to that generalization that this function cannot be located at the far left. Likewise, at about the halfway point between the center and the far right, is radio and television. In general, most ventures in ministry through radio and television can be most effectively implemented on a cooperative basis, but there are enough exceptions to that generalization that this area of ministry cannot be placed at the far right side of the spectrum.

This concept of a spectrum of tasks, functions, and services offers a frame of reference for decision-making on interchurch cooperation that may help systematize the process and reduce conflicts resulting from the mixture of motives.

Weakness or Strength?

A six-congregation cooperative ministry is formed with all congregations belonging to the same denomination. It includes three congregations with fewer than 100 members each, one 200-member congregation, one 300-member congregation, and one 1,100-member congregation. What are some probable points of tension that will arise to obstruct the process of enhancing ministry through this arrangement?

While not all will appear in every such cooperative arrangement, there is a strong probability that the following four points of tension will emerge within a relatively brief period of time.

First, the 1,100-member congregation was probably motivated to participate in this cooperative ministry because it saw opportunities to increase and enhance ministry and to accomplish tasks that could be done only by a cooperative approach. By contrast, many of the members in some of the smaller congregations probably saw this as an aid to their institutional survival and will be more concerned with keeping their institution alive than with increasing the load on their already threatened institution.

Second, some members of the three larger congregations may have seen this as an avenue to encouraging the merger or dissolution of some of the smaller congregations. Sooner or later, some members from the smaller congregations will fear that this was the original motivation for the arrangement.

Third, what should be the basis for selecting representatives to the central council? One representative per 100 members? Two representatives per congregation? Does the central council represent congregations or people?

Fourth, it will be relatively easy for the one large congregation to find very able people to represent it on this central council. On the other hand the smaller congregations have the choice of (*a*) sending "fringe members" who are not active leaders as their delegates or (*b*) overloading already heavily burdened active leaders by asking them to accept the responsibility of representing their congregation on the central council in addition to their many other responsibilities.

This illustration of what often happens in cooperative ministries is mentioned to bring out two important lessons that have relevance for both intercongregational and interdenominational ventures in cooperation.

First, the cooperative ministry that is developed from a broad base of strength will usually be stronger and far more effective than the one that is formed from a base of shared weaknesses or from a mixture of the two. Perhaps the most highly visible example of this has been in the conciliar movement. Councils of churches have been strongest and most effective when the member denominations were strong. When the member denominations were comparatively weak, the councils of churches have been weak and seriously inhibited by problems of institutional survival. The same is true at the congregational level of interchurch cooperation.

Second, it helps to reduce the number of points of potential tension if the motives for cooperation are stated and thoroughly understood. It is less important that the motives be uniform than that they be thoroughly communicated.

What Are the Lessons?

When efforts at interchurch cooperation are looked at from the perspective of decision-making, it is possible to offer several comments which may be of value to other church leaders as they embark on such ventures. These can be presented most clearly if they are divided into two sections. The longer section recounts lessons gained from experience in intercongregational cooperation, and the shorter is devoted to lessons gained from experience in the functioning of interdenominational agencies created by two or more denominational administrative units.

A. Intercongregational Cooperation

1. The first lesson in intercongregational cooperation is that past experiences have demonstrated clearly that the horizontal lines of communication and the relationships between organizations are far more difficult to build and to maintain than the vertical lines within an organization or system.

As a result most congregations find it far easier to relate to the other congregations in their own synod, or conference, or presbytery, or district, than to congregations of other denominations in their own community. Among other implications, this means that greater input and more persistence are required to build and maintain cooperative relationships with congregations of other denominations in the same community than to maintain relationships with other congregations in the same denomination, *where these relationships have been institutionalized over the years.*

Thus a cooperative arrangement including only Lutheran or only Presbyterian congregations is usually easier to develop and sustain than the cooperative arrangement that includes both Lutheran and Presbyterian churches.

A corollary of this is that the greater the number of congregations of any one denomination in an area, the easier it is for those congregations to focus on *intra*denominational cooperation and the more difficult it is for them to participate in *inter*denominational cooperation.

This is one reason why parishes of The Lutheran Church–Missouri Synod tend to be more actively involved in interchurch cooperative ventures on the East Coast than in the Midwest, and why many non-Methodists see The United Methodist Church as "noncooperative" in places where there are more United Methodist congregations than there are of any two or three other cooperative denominations put together.

2. The pastor is usually the key person in determining the degree of interchurch cooperation in which his congregation participates. In the vast majority of congregations the pastor's veto is more powerful than his influence or ability to initiate and secure support for a new course of action. Most ventures in intercongregational cooperation are built around the pastor. When he moves, retires, dies, or gets a new hobby, the cooperative arrangement is often jeopardized.

3. Laymen in every area of life tend to look at the professional in relational terms, while the professional tends to view his own role in terms of specialized skills and functions. This often leads to misunderstandings about roles, expectations, relationships, and responsibilities. Many ventures in interchurch cooperation encounter difficulties when the ministers

decide to reallocate responsibilities from the traditional pattern of the pastor as a generalist to a new pattern in which each clergyman is a specialist in one, two, or three functions of ministry. Laymen who think in terms of relationships to persons, rather than to specialists, keep asking, "But who is *our* pastor?"

4. The intercongregational cooperative arrangements which have had a comparatively long life-span (three to ten years) tend (1) to have involved a high proportion of lay leadership from the beginning and (2) to become institutionalized. Where both of these two elements have been missing, the life expectancy has tended to be short.

5. It is becoming increasingly clear that some efforts at interchurch cooperation probably should be on an ad hoc basis, should not be institutionalized, and should be allowed to die after a brief life. A frequent illustration of this is the way in which several congregations rally together in a common cause, and when this is resolved the coalition dissolves shortly afterward. The use of interchurch task forces facilitates this process.

On the other hand, many cooperative programs need continuity to be effective, and they must be institutionalized to be able to maintain this continuity. A cooperative weekday released-time program in Christian education is a common example of such a program. A council of churches is another. A third is any cooperative arrangement to provide each participating congregation with the part-time services of an ordained minister.

6. Experience suggests that the most fruitful areas for intercongregational cooperation are on issues in specialized ministries to precisely defined small segments of the total population (such as alienated street youth, persons confined to institutions, members of the confirmation class, or young single adults), in religious broadcasting, in opening up new opportunities for churchmen to participate in ministry, in the sharing of professional leadership, and in some training experiences.

The least fruitful tend to be corporate worship, Sunday School, maintenance of property, and evangelism. Any new venture in interchurch cooperation is more likely to be successful if it begins with probable "winners" rather than probable "losers."

7. Frequently major problems in efforts at interchurch cooperation are produced by one or more of three factors. The first is the issue of accountability. What is the *primary* line of accountability? To the clientele? To the source of funds? To the policy-making group? To staff? What are the *secondary* lines of accountability? A lack of clarity on this issue can be disruptive and become a major diversion from purpose and ministry.

The second factor is the temptation in many interchurch agencies to build in two lines of representation from the constituent bodies (congregations or denominational judicatories) to the cooperative agency. For example, one group of representatives may be selected by and clearly represent the constituent bodies. Another group may be selected at large by the cooperative agency in one manner or another. There is a tendency for these at-large persons to be representatives without a constituency that can hold them accountable or that can be held accountable itself.

It appears to matter little whether these two different categories of representatives are combined into one board or whether they constitute two separate boards or commissions. In either case the mere existence of these two distinctively different sets of representatives tends to become a source of disruptive and diversionary tension.

The third of these three sources of problems centers on the words *expectation* and *motivation*. Do the constituent bodies expect to receive any direct services or benefits from the cooperative agency? Does the cooperative agency expect to provide any direct services or benefits to the constituent bodies? A difference in expectations here, either in general terms or in the expectation of the specific services, can be destructive.

Some congregations enter into a cooperative ministry with the dream that this will enhance the chances of institutional survival for their church. Others come in with the expectation of saving money or reducing costs. Many come in because they expect this to enable them to reach people who may join and strengthen their congregation. Some see the cooperative ministry as designed to increase the quality of services to members. Others place the emphasis on ministry to persons who are not active members of any congregation. A lack of clarity in motivations and expectations can be both confusing and destructive.

8. There is a widespread tendency to cooperate from a position of weakness rather than from a position of strength. Congregations and denominations tend to move unilaterally when their resources and competence enable them to do so. They tend to look for allies and to be more open to cooperative approaches when it appears that their resources are not equal to the task.

One result of this tendency is that too many cooperative ministries are composed solely of small or weak congregations. A much stronger and more effective ministry often results when a careful and persistent effort was made to involve larger and stronger congregations.

9. There is an interesting and significant relationship between the size of the worshiping congregation and the tendency to become part of a cooperative ministry. A disproportionately large number of congregations in cooperative ministries tend to average *either* less than 150 *or* more than 250 at Sunday morning worship. There are proportionately few congregations actively participating in cooperative ministries which average around 200 at Sunday morning worship.

From an institutional perspective the congregation that averages 150 to 250 at Sunday morning worship is large and strong enough "to go it alone." Such a congregation has neither the urgent need to gain strength from cooperation nor the extra resources to contribute to a cooperative venture. Obviously this pattern is related to the tendency for many cooperative ministries to consist of tiny, weak congregations.

10. Finally, there has been a frequent pattern of turning to interchurch cooperation when faced with a pressing and complex challenge. Interchurch cooperation becomes a means of *avoiding* the basic issue rather than of coping with the challenge of change. This pattern can be seen in an inner-city neighborhood where most of the members of the long-established churches have moved to the suburbs. It can be seen in the hundreds of rural counties which reached their population peak in the 1920s and where today there are almost as many churches as people. It can be seen in the changing central business district of a city in the 50,000 to 250,000 population range where the economic renewal of the heart of the city is redefining the role of the large downtown congregation.

Interchurch cooperation can be a means of responding to new challenges or of avoiding the pressure to face reality. It is not necessary for everyone to reinvent the wheel—these lessons from experience can be helpful to any congregation if it is about to embark on a new venture in interchurch cooperation.

B. Interdenominational Agencies

When two or more denominations cooperate to create a new interchurch agency that agency can avoid many unnecessary problems by reflecting on the following lessons.

From the perspective of the interdenominational agency the most important lesson is the same lesson that applies to pastors and to regional judicatories: *Service the clientele.*

James Glasse contends that a pastor should plan to "pay his rent" every week by attending to his basic responsibilities in three areas—personal, professional, and institutional. Glasse suggests that a pastor can "pay his rent" every week and still have two or three or four days "left over" for discretionary interests and activities.[2] The same point applies to interdenominational agencies. If the agency will pay its rent regularly, it has time for other agenda items.

The second lesson is: *Identify the clientele.*

Many interdenominational and interfaith agencies have two or three sets of "clients." Recently, for example, several denominations banded together to create and finance an agency to be concerned with the twin issues of prison reform and the criminal justice system. Who constitutes the clientele of this agency? There are at least three sets of clients. One set is composed of the persons and institutions directly involved in the administration of the whole criminal justice system, including the prisons and the persons in prison. This set may be divided into two or three subdivisions, including the people administering the system, the prisoners and other "victims" of the system, and the governmental agencies financing the operation of the system. A second clientele consists of the allies and potential allies from reform groups interested in changing the system. The third set of clients consists of the denominations paying the cost of establishing and maintaining the offices. There may be a fourth set of clients, consisting of the members of the governing or advisory board of the agency.

The third lesson is closely related to the first two: *Identify the agenda of the clientele.* Unless this has been done it is impossible to service the clientele. The temptation in every interdenominational agency (and in all other institutions in society) is for the staff to develop its own agenda and respond to that agenda. This is normal and natural. It is also suicidal unless (a) that agenda coincides with the agenda of the clientele or (b) that agenda is carried out *after* the rent has been paid.

A fourth lesson in the administration of interchurch agencies is relatively simple: *Report to the clientele.* This means informing each set of clients on a regular basis about what has happened, what is happening, and what is proposed for the future. It is especially important to keep open the channels of communication with the denominations paying the bills.

The interdenominational agency that takes seriously these four lessons from past experience will have relatively few diversionary problems about finances, administration, or lack of denominational interest. It will also have adequate time and energy to devote both to its purpose and to the various sets of clientele. The interdenominational agency that ignores all four lessons, and especially the first three, will have serious financial problems, an excessive amount of time devoted to fund-raising, many dissatisfied persons among the denominational supporters, and a disenchanted staff. Examples of this can be found among the so-called ecumenical campus ministries at scores of universities all across the country.

7 Dollars and Decisions

"I was really surprised," exclaimed a former editor of *Life* after that magazine had folded and she had failed to be hired for another position with Time, Inc. "We were all brought up to think good old Uncle Time, Inc. would take care of our spiritual and bodily needs forever." [1]

"Maybe it makes economic sense to contract out the cleaning of an office building to a private company," said the gray-haired pastor of First Presbyterian Church, "but a church is different. We have to have our own custodian on duty here. It simply wouldn't work to set up a joint arrangement for janitorial services among these four downtown churches. I suppose that might be one way to cut costs, but what will we do without our own custodian when one of the ladies calls at 8:30 in the morning for Charlie to put the coffee pot on for their 9 A.M. meeting or someone else calls in the late afternoon to have chairs set up for an evening meeting?"

" But we've always had our own minister!" exclaimed the wife of the leading layman in the 57-member Cumberland Presbyterian Church in rural Tennessee. "We've been members here for over forty years and we've always had our own minister. I don't see why we should be expected to share a minister with some other church! Does every minister have to have a big salary? Don't we have any ministers left who want to preach because they love the Lord?"

These three comments reflect one of the most important pressures on the decision-making process in the churches. Frequently this is described simply as the pressure of rising costs. While that is true, it is not sufficiently precise to be an adequate description of the problem.

The basic generalization that describes this pressure more adequately is that the cost of person-centered services is rising faster than the increases, if any, in productivity. The churches, along with magazine publishers, hospitals, department stores, schools, museums, municipal police departments, newspapers, and theological seminaries, are among the many organizations in our society in which dollars are having an increasing influence on decisions.

Several denominations, for example, are recognizing the value of an intentional interim pastorate by an experienced minister. Among the situations in which an intentional interim pastorate can be very helpful are (1) when a greatly beloved pastor dies in tragic circumstances, (2) following the death or retirement of a minister who has served that same congregation for twenty or thirty years, (3) following the departure of a minister who left under a cloud because of alcoholism, the misuse of church funds, or involvement with a woman other than his wife, and (4) when the departure of a minister coincides with the end of a long period of stability and the church has to adapt to rapid changes in the community. [2]

Given the value of an intentional interim pastorate of six to twenty-four months in a growing number of situations where there is a pulpit vacancy, what are the factors that should influence the choice and tenure of the interim pastor? The needs of the congregation? The experienced judgment of the chief executive officer of the regional judicatory, such as the synod president or a district superintendent or a bishop? Those considerations which will help the next permanent pastor have an effective ministry in the parish? The relationship of the parish with neighboring congregations?

In most denominations the most influential factors in the selection, tenure, and role of an interim pastor for the congregation temporarily without its own minister are:

1. The desire by both congregation and denominational leaders to get the pulpit filled with a permanent minister as soon as possible and thus (*a*) end the uncertainty and (*b*) cross that "problem" off the list

2. The rules and regulations of the denominational pension fund

3. The restrictions on the income of persons receiving Social Security benefits
4. The geographical location of the congregation
5. The availability and ego needs of ministers not serving parishes
6. The desire of the congregation to save a few thousand dollars
7. The advice of the regional denominational executive
8. The needs of the congregation during the interim between pastors
9. The relationship of the congregation with neighboring parishes

Two of the first three factors on that list, and three of the first six, are financial considerations!

While more highly visible in some cases than in others, economic and financial considerations are increasingly influential in the decision-making processes of the churches. The reasons for this, and the prospects for the future, can be seen more clearly by examining in more detail four different dimensions of this issue. The first suggests a basic reason for the increasing impact of financial considerations, the second suggests one means of turning this financial squeeze into a creative analysis of ministry, the third forecasts a trend that may radically change how churches finance certain programs and ministers, while the fourth raises serveral questions that may be helpful in the allocation of financial resources.

The Seven-Percent Crunch

As was suggested earlier, the basic generalization that helps explain why economic considerations are increasingly important in decision-making in the churches can be stated in one sentence: The cost of person-centered services is rising faster that the increase in productivity.

Today it is possible to buy a better radio for ten dollars than one could purchase for fifteen dollars in 1950, despite the decrease in the buying power of the dollar over the past quarter-century. The same statement can be made about a long list of other manufactured products, such as watches, cameras, freezers, and tires.

By contrast the cost of such person-centered services as one day's care in a hospital, one year's education at a college, university, or theological seminary, a month's work by a social worker, six meals served by one waitress, an eye examination, an hour of an attorney's time, a week of police protection, or a hospital call by a minister have increased three to ten times during the past quarter-century.

This rapid increase in the cost of person-centered services has produced a strong negative reaction in a society which concentrated for decades on the production of goods, and in which annual increases in productivity were expected and realized and largely offset increases in wages and salaries.

How does one achieve an increase in the productivity of a minister preparing a sermon, of a newspaper reporter covering a flood, of a first baseman catching a pop fly, of a lawyer drawing up a will, of a surgeon performing an operation, of a nurse supplying eight hours of care for a critically ill patient, of the teacher of a fifth-grade class, or of an author writing a book? In each case annual increases in wages and salaries exceed any possible increase in productivity.

Though in many cases there may have been significant increases in the *quality* of the service, at least as often the unit costs, in terms of hours of time invested, have increased. For example, many pastors now find it takes more time to make a hospital call, since their hospitalized members are scattered among a larger number of hospitals than was true in 1953 or 1965.

The crunch is especially acute in many Protestant churches, since, unlike the price of newspapers or the cost of a day in the hospital or the tax rate for the local schools, receipts have risen at a relatively slow rate during the current inflationary period that began back in 1964. In the inflationary period of

1950–55 related to the Korean War, per member giving increased by 40 to 50 percent in most denominations while per capita personal income increased by 22 percent during the same period.

From 1961 through 1973 take-home pay for members of the labor force rose at the rate of 6.2 percent per year. This means that after the effect of compounding this annual rate is taken into account, the 1973 take-home pay for the average member of the labor force was double the 1961 level. How many congregations or denominations doubled their total receipts between 1961 and 1973? Since 1965 the per capita disposable income for the entire American population has risen at an annual rate of 8 percent per year.

In brief, what has happened is that for several years the costs of person-centered services have been rising from a low of 6 percent per year in some fields to 12 percent per year in the other areas. The costs of operating theological seminaries, for example, have risen at an average rate of 10 percent per year for the past decade.

Likewise, on a national basis, local property taxes have been rising at a rate of 10 percent per year. On a per pupil basis public school costs increased at the rate of nearly 10 percent per year from 1961 through 1973.

This means that the organization producing person-centered services is caught in the crunch of trying to cover costs that are rising at the rate of 6 to 12 percent per year while serving a population that has had an increase in after-tax income of 6 to 8 percent per person per year.

As a result, almost without exception, *the organization producing person-centered services that has not had an increase in its annual receipts averaging at least 7 percent per year is in trouble* and has to choose among four difficult alternatives.

The churches and other organizations providing person-centered services that are caught in the "seven-percent crunch" have four basic alternatives.

1. Cut quantity.

One alternative is to reduce the quantity of services available. Schools may cut out special classes and thus reduce the number of staff. Many churches and judicatories have followed this same course of action and have reduced the number of paid staff and reduced program and services.

2. Cut quality.

A second and related alternative is to reduce quality. The third-grade teacher may have 36 instead of 29 pupils, or may be asked to teach music in addition to other duties instead of relying on a specially trained teacher of music. Likewise many churches have reduced the quality of certain ministries in order to cut costs.

3. Develop a new approach.

One of the most common examples of a new approach is the congregation which for several decades was served by a full-time pastor and now is served by a minister who also serves as the chaplain at a nearby institution, or is in school, or serves another congregation. Another is the response to people eating out that has been developed by the "fast food" entrepreneurs.

4. Increase receipts.

Increasing receipts was the alternative chosen by most churches in the inflationary period of 1950–55 and during the past decade by hospitals, the post office, schools, major league baseball and football teams, restaurants, newspapers, and some churches. Most churches and regional judicatories, however, have operated on the premise that they would "make do" on the basis of increases in annual receipts averaging 2 or 3 or 4 percent per year. After several years of following this alternative many of them are now feeling the cumulative impact. They will have to face up to the need for a sharp increase in receipts or other major changes, one of which may be to go out of business. (In 1971, 1972, and 1973 a remarkably large number of congregations shifted from a defensive posture to a more aggressive approach and in the space of a year or two raised the level of giving by 30 to 50 percent.)

The consequences of this crunch can be seen all across the churches. The financial support by the churches in the United States for work of the Christian church around the world has hit a plateau in several denominations. This means that *in terms of the buying power of the dollar* on other continents, after allowing for the impact of inflation and devaluation, the churches in the United States are giving only 50 to 80 percent as much for overseas work as they gave back in 1964.

What has this meant to the churches? It has meant in The United Presbyterian Church, The United Methodist Church, and other denominations a dollar cut in the amount allocated for theological education. It meant that an unprecedented number of seminaries began to budget deficits for their projections into the future.

It also means that for the past several years pastors' salaries have not been keeping pace with increases in the income level of the general population. In one district in The American Lutheran Church, for example, the average salary of pastors rose from $5,848 in 1967 to $7,875 in 1972, an increase of 35 percent. During that same period the per capita disposable (after taxes) personal income of the American people increased by 44 percent!

It also means that many congregations are being "priced out of the ministerial market." Thus, as the supply of ministers has increased, the number of jobs has decreased. In the Lutheran Church in America, for example, the number of ministers increased from 6,842 in 1962 to 7,691 in 1971, but the number of positions for clergymen decreased. During the 1960s The United Presbyterian Church added 1,182 clergymen but the number of congregations decreased by 523, while in the Episcopal Church there was a net increase of 2,647 clergymen and a net decrease in congregations of 588.

Thus for many churches and for most of the larger Protestant denominations the seven-percent crunch has increased the impact of financial considerations on a wide range of decisions. Another result has been that an increasing number of leaders in the churches have become convinced that costs must be examined more carefully. This is in sharp contrast to the pattern of the early 1950s, when the basic response to rising costs was to go out and increase receipts.[3]

Benefits and Costs

"That was a good sermon, Reverend," commented a gray-haired man in his late forties as he shook hands with his pastor after the morning worship service one Sunday. "But I am not sure it was worth $100."

What did he mean? Who can determine whether a sermon is worth $50 or $100 or $500? What kind of church would create the conditions that could lead to such a comment?

This episode occurred in a congregation that uses a "program" budget as one of its basic planning tools. In the fall of 1970 the finance committee initiated the practice of preparing two expenditrue budgets for the coming church year. The first was in the usual "input" or expenditure form, and listed such categories as salaries, pensions, insurance, taxes, office supplies, postage, maintenance, utilities. debt retirement, local outreach, and benevolences. These are the categories into which the money from the church treasury flowed.

The second was a "program" or "output" budget and used three general categories for expenditures. Under the first, "ministry to the members," were listed such program areas as Sunday morning worship, education and nurture, pastoral care, lay training programs, special celebrations, and fellowship. Another general category was labeled "ministry to persons in this community beyond the membership." Under it were such programs as the day care center for the children of working mothers, ministry to alcoholics and their families, ministry on community issues, evangelism, and a half dozen other items.

The last of these three general categories was titled "ministry to persons outside this community," and here more than fifty individual items were listed. This was the equivalent of the item called "benevolences" or "missions" in the traditional expenditure budget and included the various denominational askings as well as other benevolences.

The gray-haired man who made the evaluative comment to the pastor is a federal employee with a master's degree in operations research. He, the local municipal budget analyst, five other members, and the minister had comprised the committee that developed a program budget for the church. They agreed that it would be more meaningful to the membership if the annual budget could be presented in terms of the program or ministry that was being financed rather than in terms of the goods and services that were being purchased.

As the first part of the process they developed a "performance budget," in which they calculated the estimated costs of each program component. When they came to the minister's time, they found that after adding together his cash salary, housing costs, travel costs, pension, fees for continuing education, insurance premiums, the denominational expenses related to having a minister including denominational support of theological education and the cost of ministerial placement, the cost of providing him with an office, and half of the cost of having a full-time secretary (the other half was charged to other areas of program), it cost $9 for each hour of his *productive* time that he was able to allocate to the life and work of that congregation.

Two members of the congregation were appalled when they heard the church was paying the pastor $9 an hour. They thought this was an exorbitant figure. The operations research specialist and the budget analyst quickly pointed out that this was a misunderstanding. In the first place, they emphasized, that is *not* what the church is paying the minister. That is what it costs for each hour of his *productive* time Typically, this cost is 50 to 200 percent higher than the actual dollar compensation received by the person. It is a concept used in setting fee schedules that is widely used in medical clinics, automobile repair shops, law offices, consulting firms, educational institutions, and many businesses. Second, $9 an hour is a comparatively low figure for a professional person. The gross cost of each productive hour of the typical professional's time frequently runs between $20 and $50. One reason it is so low in the local church is that the typical minister works many hours each week, supervisory costs are remarkably low, and office overhead is usually very modest.

During the course of the preparation of the program budget, the minister reported that typically he spent ten to twelve hours a week preparing his sermon for Sunday morning. Out of this came the approximation of $100 as the cost of preparing each sermon, $300 for the total cost of each corporate worship service (most of the $300 was the imputed rent of the physical facilities), and $6 for each hospital call. After developing these unit costs—which, incidentally, were *not* publicized among the members—it was possible to estimate the total costs for each program area.

This congregation is involved in one of the most rapidly growing management practices in the nation today, a trend which will have a major impact on the decision-making process in a wide range of ecclesiastical organizations, including the local church, during the 1970s. This is the use of the budget as a basic tool for planning program, for setting priorities, for resolving conflict, and for self-evaluation. When used in this manner, the budget also becomes a very useful channel for internal communication in the organization. The adoption of this management practice requires the organization to identify the cost of goods and services which normally do not carry a highly visible price tag. One result is that organizations using this approach to decision-making can identify the costs of each component of their program and these "price tags" are very useful in choosing among alternatives.

An example of this can be seen by looking at the question, What will $100 buy in today's marketplace?

While costs do vary from organization to organization and from region to region, it is possible to illustrate the value of that question and to suggest a few of the implications of this approach to planning and decision-making.

Today $100 will buy one reasonably well-prepared sermon in a 700-member congregation, or one day of care in the nearby university hospital, or twenty to thirty completed home visits by the pastor, or the necessary subsidy to fifty to one hundred subscribers to the denominational magazine, or the teaching time of one seminary professor for one hour in a seminary classroom, or one day of instruction for twenty-five sixth-graders in the public school, or a half-day visit by a denominational executive to a local church, or two to four hours of a good attorney's time, or the cost of one overloaded case-worker's time with one family for one year in the local public welfare agency, or the full cost of the use of the new church kitchen for one evening.

These examples illustrate and support the reaction of consumers in all segments of the economy—$100 certainly does not buy very much today!

There are many different reasons for the growing interest in this form of program budgeting and cost accounting, and most of these reasons have a high degree of relevance to the decision-making process in the local church and in ecclesiastical organizations.

High on this list of reasons is a widespread shift in American society in the direction of a greater emphasis on "user charges." For several decades the national trend has been to pay for services out of a general fund collected with very limited attention to the direct benefits received by the contributors to that fund. During the past ten or fifteen years the trend has begun to move in the other direction. Today, owing in part to the increased use of hospitalization insurance, the typical hospital patient pays a larger percentage of the actual cost of his care than was the case in 1955. There is a rapidly growing wave of public opinion urging the development of a system that will enable the university student to repay the cost of his education out of future earnings. The ecology movement has sparked a demand that the consumer should pay for the ultimate disposal of glass bottles, aluminum cans, yesterday's newspaper, and junked automobiles. The recent tremendous increase in private security systems to supplement the local police force is financed by user benefit charges. Municipalities, public school districts, and state and national parks are being forced to turn to user charges for a larger share of their revenues as they respond to a taxpayers' revolt. The toll roads that were constructed in the 1950s and the use of a highway trust fund to finance the interstate highway system represent other examples of this concept. Amtrak is based on the assumption that passenger train service can and should pay its own way. The recent reorganization of the postal service as a quasi-public agency was based on the belief that users of the mails should pay the costs of that service. The rapid rise in tuition costs in private colleges is another expression of this trend. The growing opposition in several denominations to continuing the use of denominational funds to supplement the salary of pastors of small congregations also reflects the user-benefit concept.

A second factor is the recent rapid rise in the cost of person-centered services such as health care, education, welfare, recreation, counseling, and religion. As was pointed out in the previous section, the gains in productivity that have been achieved in the production of food, fiber, and mass-produced manufactured goods have not been matched by equivalent increases in the quantitative productivity of person-centered services. During the past three decades, the number of employees per 100 students has gone up, not down, in most public school systems. The number of employee hours required per day of patient care has increased tremendously in hospitals, as has the number of persons employed to run the current jerry-built welfare system. The number of professional staff persons directly employed by the churches for each 1,000 members has doubled in twenty-five years, and the number of denominational staff members has tripled in thirty-five years. While it can be argued that the quality of the services has increased, that does not alter the fact that the unit cost of these services has been increasing whereas the unit cost of many manufactured products has dropped despite an increase in quality.

This continued increase in unit costs for person-centered services has sparked a demand for detailed explanations of why costs keep rising. This in turn has led to the application of cost accounting techniques in organizations where previously the emphasis was on income rather than expenditures. A simple illustration of this is the recent public comparisons that have been made between Yale University, where the response to rising costs has traditionally been to seek additional revenues, and the University of Southern California, where there has been a tradition of keeping expenditures under control. Today, Yale is engaged in pioneering efforts to control costs and is developing cost accounting procedures to evaluate alternative approaches to educational administration.

Perhaps the most important of all the contemporary factors behind the current wave of interest in analyzing an organization's budget in terms of program costs is the emergence of a new system of decision-making. The most widely known example of this is called Planning-Programming-Budgeting-System (PPBS or PPB). This was developed in the Department of Defense under Secretary Robert S. McNamara, and in 1965 President Johnson ordered all federal departments to start using it. Although PPB has had a stormy career—many people have dropped the first two initials in describing it, and the federal government terminated its mandatory use in 1971—the basic concept has been widely adopted.[4]

In very simple terms, PPB is a means of combining into one process planning and goal-setting, program development, the ordering of priorities in the allocation of resources (budgeting), and a built-in basis for subsequent self-evaluation. The basic reason for development and acceptance of the concept was that it was seen as a means of moving away from a simple repetitive system of financing permanent bureaucracies and toward a systematic method of making the budget reflect the priorities in the purpose and program of an agency.

This process enables the persons responsible for making and implementing decisions to deal with costs and probable consequences as well as with goals and policies. It also greatly facilitates a holistic approach to the purpose and program of an organization, and this may be one of the reasons why it is attracting the interest of a growing number of church leaders.

Several denominations are now using adaptations of PPB at the national administrative level. In some, the system is built around three words—*planning, budgeting,* and *evaluation,* as these administrative tools are combined into one process. In every case, the system, regardless of name, combines multi-year budgeting, an improved information system for making both tactical and strategic decisions, planning, cost-benefit analysis, and other evaluation tools. One denomination has developed a four-tier system consisting of purpose, aims, program, and program components or activities. When this outline is used to describe the work of a board or commission, it helps the decision-makers to choose among alternatives, since each activity can be viewed in terms of probable costs and anticipated benefits in addition to its relationship to the basic purpose of the organization and to the total program of that board.

What are the implications for the churches? How will the use of the planning-programming-budgeting concept be felt in the churches? What will be the impact of the application of the cost-benefit theory to ecclesiastical organizations? How will the growing emphasis on the user charge concept affect the churches?

A few of the initial responses can be seen already in the closing of many Catholic and Lutheran parochial schools, in the various proposals to merge theological seminaries, in the reduction of denominational staffs, in the rejection of proposals for local church building projects that would have won enthusiastic support fifteen years ago, in the financial crisis facing over 200 church-related colleges, and in the recent demise of several denominational publications.

While it is easy to read too much into these changes, to varying degrees every one does represent an application of the cost-benefit formula. In addition, in each case the crisis that led to the change was precipitated, at least in part, by the unwillingness or inability of the users to pay the full cost of the services received.

The impact of this growing emphasis on costs may be greater in the churches than in other segments of society because of the manner in which costs have been handled in religious organizations. Judging by current practices, it appears that church members are willing to pay directly the full cost for groceries, drugs, motion pictures, dental services, use of a toll road, telephone service, electricity, books, private camps, church buildings, pastoral services, and perhaps television broadcasts, but are unwilling to accept direct full-cost user charges for the denominational magazine, a week at summer church camp, denominational staff services, parochial schools (which in part are heavily subsidized by the comparatively low salaries paid to staff and faculty), lay training programs, pensions for ministers, cooperative ministries, and job placement services for clergy. The resolution of this paradox is at the heart of the financial squeeze on denominational and interdenominational agencies. One approach to the problem is to emphasize a reduction in costs by reducing services. Another is to attempt to solve it by restructure (see chapter 5). A third is to increase the level of income.

Perhaps the most highly visible current result of the new awareness of costs is that increasingly, in both denominational judicatories and local churches, the budget is being used as the primary arena for resolving conflict within the organization. (This, incidentally, was one of the causes of the demise of PPB in the federal government.) Unlike profit-making corporations, which can still turn to the marketplace for the resolution of conflict, or governmental organizations, which place a heavy dependence on elections and referenda in resolving conflict, nonprofit organizations have few better alternatives than the budget for dealing with conflict situations.[5] The most widely publicized example of the budget as the arena for conflict over purpose and policies was in the Episcopal Church between 1968 and 1972, when several dioceses drastically reduced the amount pledged to the national agencies in the preparation of the diocesan budget.

This same trend is evident in the local church. In one Presbyterian congregation, for example, three budgets were presented at a congregational meeting. One was the budget recommended by a majority of the finance committee, based on an optimistic view of anticipated receipts. The second was prepared by a minority of that committee who were much more pessimistic about the projected income figures. The third was submitted as an amendment to the finance committee's recommendation by a dissident group who used this approach in the hope of securing what would be, in effect, a vote of no confidence in the professional staff. While the polity of the denomination does not require the budget to be submitted to a congregational vote, the informal decision by all leadership groups to use the proposed budget as a means of resolving the conflict within the organization meant that the congregation had to vote on the proposed budget.

A second manifestation of the influence of dollars on decision-making is also rapidly gaining visibility. This is the shift toward a greater reliance on part-time or temporary employees rather than on creating or filling full-time staff positions. This trend has been accelerated by the increasing demand for highly specialized staff services and also by the income-expense squeeze being felt in many congregations and denominational agencies. In an era when the increase in church receipts often does not match the decrease in the buying power of the dollar, this is an attractive alternative. For example, a local church may decide to hire someone locally on a part-time basis at $3.50 an hour, or $2,000 a year, to serve as director of Christian education or as minister of youth. This idea becomes even more attractive when a careful analysis of all costs reveals that the actual total cost of another full-time staff person is double the proposed $7,500 salary. The financial squeeze encourages local church leaders to look more carefully at both costs and benefits when considering additional staff. This new openness toward the use of part-time or temporary employees can also be seen in the staffing of denominational judicatories and interdenominational agencies. Perhaps the most common illustration is in staffing training programs and special task forces or study committees.

One of the most interesting results of the use of program budgeting is that it is bringing together two types of church leaders who frequently in the past have not been able to communicate effectively with one another. One type is exemplified by the individual who wants to look at the administration of the church from the perspective of "the hardheaded businessman who knows the value of a dollar." The other type is represented by the person who insists, "The church is not in business to make money or to save money; the business of the church is ministry to people!"

Both types are finding that a program budget which includes a breakdown of the unit costs of each program component is a valuable tool. In the past it was often the case that the "hardheaded businessman" type dominated the budget preparation process while the individual who found the budget a dull but necessary instrument concentrated his energies on program planning and development. In many congregations

159

and in most regional judicatories, however, the end result was that the "hardheaded businessman" was in charge of both budgeting and program planning, since financial limitations determined program. The use of the planning-programming-budgeting process brings these two types together as program planning and budget preparation are merged into a single process. In this process it becomes clear that the operational definition of purpose and the actual priorities of the congregation are presented more clearly in the budget than anywhere else in the life of that organization.

To be more specific, this approach to local church administration tends to make obsolete the traditional finance committee, it tends to improve the level of accountability, it tends to increase the degree of intentionality and precision in the allocation of resources, and it provides a common agenda for those who are primarily concerned about mission and those who are inclined to believe the church neglects the economic facts of life.[6]

While these developments are both interesting and significant, from a long-term perspective it may be that the most important contributions of these administrative tools can be summarized with two words—*innovation* and *evaluation*.

A possible example of the former can be seen in the education of seminary students. In 1960 the typical cost of the theological education of a seminary graduate was approximately $10,000 to $12,000. Today it is in the neighborhood of $25,000 in many theological seminaries, and in several each graduate carries a "price tag" of over $30,000. It appears that a continuation of present styles of theological education and financial trends will raise this cost figure to $50,000 per graduate by 1980.

What does that mean?

If one assumes that the ultimate "consumer" is the religious organization that employs these graduates, and if one assumes that the average graduate will spend twenty-five years in the professional ministry, this means that the employer should be putting $1,000 a year into a "ministerial depreciation fund" to pay for the education of replacements for the present clergy staff. If costs were presented in this form, it would probably encourage a change either in the allocation of ministerial manpower or in the method of providing a theological education for ministers. Inasmuch as many changes and innovations tend to be the result of pressures from outside the organization, this would be one method of encouraging innovation. The combination of careful cost analysis, a rapidly growing emphasis on performance and quality, and the emerging trend in the United States of turning to *ad hoc* groups, individuals, and private agencies for many of the tasks traditionally performed by established bureaucracies, may accelerate the pace of innovation in theological education tremendously during the 1970s. This analogy can be extended to campus ministries, church groups, publications, and many other programs and ministries of the church in addition to theological education. The magazine *A.D.*, which began as a joint publication of the United Church of Christ and The United Presbyterian Church, is one example of innovation as a result of financial pressures.

The demand for more effective and meaningful evaluation of program and ministry is one of the fastest growing trends in the churches today. The planning-programming-budgeting process provides what may turn out to be the most helpful response to that demand.

Recently a mission board was hearing requests for financial grants. Two of these were from church-sponsored nursery schools. Each was being supported very vigorously with strong emotional appeals by their respective proponents. As they listened to the pleas for money it was difficult for the board members to decide which was the more meritorious. Finally one board member, who had been listening very intently and examining the written presentations with great care, said, "As I try to understand these two presentations I am unable to distinguish any qualitative difference between the two programs." As he said this, the other board members and the representatives from the two groups nodded in agreement. "What puzzles me, however," he continued, "is that at Grace Church the costs average out to $.87 per child per hour, while at Trinity the costs average out to $1.94 per child per hour. Unless someone can explain this huge difference in costs, I think I know which one I am going to suggest should receive the higher priority in the allocation of our very limited funds."

The application of the cost-benefit concept, which is an essential element of the planning-programming-budgeting process, can be useful in strengthening the decision-making processes in the churches.

As this concept becomes more prevalent it may be that one Sunday morning a few years hence a pastor may be greeted with this comment after a Sunday morning worship service: "Reverend, I find your $150 sermons to be five times as helpful as your $100 ones."

Who Gets the Subsidy?

Another very important financial trend that will have a major impact on the decision-making processes of the churches is related to costs in general, and to subsidies in particular. In the previous section it was pointed out that, as part of the emphasis on relating costs to benefits, there is a marked trend in the direction of expecting the consumer to pay the full cost of the service received. Not all consumers of services, however, can pay the full cost of providing that service. As a result an elaborate system of subsidies has developed in American society. Conspicuous examples of this include "free" public schools, "free" public libraries, free city streets and country roads (as contrasted with toll roads), free public parks, partially subsidized mass transit, and free parking at the shopping center. In each case the consumer does not pay the full direct cost as he does when he mails a first-class letter or plays a round of golf at a new private club or turns on an electric light or makes a long-distance telephone call.

This system of subsidies is also operative in the churches. A seminary student does not pay the full cost of his theological education; in most cases an individual congregation does not pay the full cost of a lecture by a missionary on furlough; the resident in a church-sponsored home for the elderly does not pay the full cost of living there; the seven-year-old in a church school does not pay the full cost of that fifty-minute session once a week; and most congregations do not pay the full cost of the denominational placement service (or, to be more precise, personnel system) that helps them secure a replacement for the minister who recently moved, died, or retired.

In each of the examples cited in the two preceding paragraphs a subsidy, or in many cases a series of subsidies, has been provided *to the organization, agency, or institution producing that service.*

In recent years a major shift has begun to occur in this system of subsidies. *The trend now is clearly in the direction of subsidizing the recipient of that service.*

The origins of this trend can be seen in the G. I. Bill of World War II, which provided subsidies to veterans who wanted to attend school. The basic financial grant went to the veteran, who channeled it to the educational institution of his choice. This concept has been adopted in state scholarship programs adopted by over half the states and marks a radical departure from the previous pattern of using state funds only for public institutions of higher education. Now state funds can be directed to private colleges and universities by routing the subsidy via the consumer of the educational services.

During the past two decades a growing number of programs have emerged which direct the subsidy to the consumer of the service rather than to the producers. A few of the federal subsidies to agriculture have been changed over the years to subsidize the consumer of the produce rather than the long line of producers. The most highly visible current example is food stamps.

The Housing Act of 1968 began the process of changing the

system of federal subsidies for housing. Sections 235 and 236 of that act provided subsidies to the consumers of housing services. This contrasts with thirty-five years of public housing, and with Sections 202, 221, 231, and other earlier subsidies that were directed at helping the producer of housing for low-income persons.

By 1980 most of the federal and state subsidies for housing persons who cannot afford the marketplace price of housing will probably be in the form of grants and income supplements to the consumers of housing rather than to the producers.

Other examples of this change in philosophy include Medicare, Social Security, Aid to Dependent Children, and burial benefits for veterans. In each case the subsidy is directed at the consumer of the service, not at the producer.[7]

Perhaps the most important step in the reinforcing of this new trend was the 1972 federal aid to higher education. Despite the objections of the presidents and other representatives from such schools as Harvard, Boston University, the University of Rhode Island, MIT, Wellesley, Holy Cross, and many others, the view of Senator Claiborne Pell (D-Rhode Island) prevailed. He stated the issue very clearly when he asked, "Will federal policy be focused on people, on youngsters and their needs, or will it focus primarily on the needs of institutions?"

In contrast to this growing trend in the public sector to subsidize the consumer of services, the pattern in the churches has been, and still is, overwhelmingly on the side of directly subsidizing the producer of services rather than the consumer. There are a few exceptions to this generalization, such as a limited number of scholarships to foreign students or to persons from a minority group, a few churches which make direct appropriations to retired ministers instead of channeling these grants through a denominational pension board, and some forms of salary supplement which are directed to the congregation rather than to the pastor.

In general, however, the churches continue to make their

annual appropriations of money in a form which subsidizes the producer of the services, rather than the consumer. Examples of this include the annual appropriations to church-related hospitals, homes, community centers, colleges, seminaries, camps, denominational periodicals, pension boards, regional staff, councils of churches, continuing education programs, and cooperative ministries.

This picture is beginning to change, however. The most highly visible change is in the denominational and local church subsidies for the continuing education of pastors. Increasingly these grants are being made directly to the pastor, and he can choose the time, place, and program that appear to meet his needs. There are also scattered instances of denominational grants being redirected to the congregations which are part of some form of cooperative ministry, rather than being sent directly to the headquarters of the cooperative ministry. Many denominations have also begun to make grants directly to the poor, the oppressed, the downtrodden, and the members of minority groups, rather than to the agencies which traditionally have existed to provide services to these people.

What would happen if the churches made a parallel shift in the policies underlying denominational grants and subsidies?

It would mean that instead of annual grants to denominational theological seminaries the churches would provide vouchers worth $2,000 to $7,000 each to seminary students. The students would pick the seminary they wanted to attend and turn the vouchers in toward their bill for tuition, books, room, and board.

It would mean that instead of subsidizing the operation of a church camp the regional judicatory would divide that amount of money among the prospective campers and issue vouchers good for $10 or $25 or $50 per camper and the camper could pick his camp from a list of approved operations.

It would mean that instead of an annual subsidy of perhaps $50,000 to a home for the elderly the regional judicatory would offer a series of "scholarships" to elderly persons in need of decent housing.

It would mean that instead of the $25,000 annual subsidy to the school of nursing run by the denominational hospital there might be twenty-five $1,000 scholarships to prospective students in financial need.

It would mean that instead of providing "free" consultative services by denominational staff to congregations the denomination would pay between one-fourth and perhaps three-fourths of the cost to a congregation involved in securing an outside consultant.

It would mean that instead of subsidizing the producers of continuing education programs for ministers the denomination would offer vouchers to ministers each year. The pastors could pick the place and type of continuing education they believed they needed and, if necessary, save up their vouchers for two or three or four years to pay the cost. (This is already beginning to happen.)

It would mean that instead of subsidizing the operation of a community center in a poverty neighborhood the denomination would make funds available to be used by the consumers of these services and they could buy the services they felt they needed from whatever source was available.

If this concept of subsidizing the consumer rather than the producer of services gains support as rapidly in the churches as it has in other segments of society, it will produce radical changes in the decision-making processes in ecclesiastical organizations, only a few of which can be foreseen.

As with every other change, this one has price tags attached to it. Perhaps the largest is the problem of quality control. This has turned out to be a major issue in recent efforts to direct the subsidy to the low-income consumer of housing under Sections 235 and 236 of the Housing Act of 1968. It is also a problem in Medicare and in several forms of public assistance. In each case there has been difficulty in policing the program to insure that the consumer gets full value for each dollar expended.

Closely related to this is the problem of accountability. When the grants are directed to the producer of services, rather than to the consumer, it is far easier to maintain adequate lines of accountability. An outstanding recent illustration of this is described by Richard W. Poston in *The Gang and the Establishment*, an account of how "consumer-oriented" grants to street gangs to attack ghetto problems turned into a fascinating "hustle" of the Establishment by gangs.

On the other side of the ledger are three important considerations. The first is that this approach is consistent with the growing anti-bureaucratic sentiment of the day. The second is that subsidizing the consumer directly is one means of making the producers of services pay more careful attention to costs. When the subsidy comes directly to the producer of services, the temptation for the administrator of the agency is to focus more attention on raising money than on keeping costs down.

Far more important in the long run, however, is the third consideration—the mounting evidence that this trend toward subsidizing the consumer rather than the producer of services is compatible with the growing demand for participatory democracy, with the rapidly accelerating trend toward granting the client a greater voice in the making of the policies that affect his destiny, and with the dawning realization that people can no longer be managed as they could be ten or twenty or fifty years ago.

Criteria in the Allocation of Resources

The cumulative impact of (1) the seven-percent crunch, (2) the increasing attention to analyzing fiscal decisions in terms of anticipated benefits and probable costs, (3) the shift in the direction of subsidizing the consumer rather than the producer of services, (4) the variety of other efforts to improve the quality of decision-making processes in the churches, and (5) the swing toward decentralization, may be felt more in the regional judicatories than in either the congregations or the national agencies of the churches. Perhaps this issue can be stated more clearly in the form of a question: As it allocates its financial resources, how can a regional judicatory, such as a diocese or synod or conference or association, improve the quality of this process? How can the people charged with the responsibility for setting the priorities improve the quality of their work?

One response to this question is to develop a set of criteria reflecting the priorities of the judicatory. Another is to incorporate these criteria into a series of questions to be asked of those seeking funds for various programs, projects, and ministries. The list of questions presented here is intended to suggest the type of questions that might be asked. Obviously each regional judicatory will have to develop its own list to reflect the values, criteria, and priorities of that synod or conference or convention or district.

1. When, how, why, and for how much money did this get into the judicatory budget originally? How has the current purpose changed from the original justification? Why? Has the dollar amount changed? How much? Why?

2. Is this *primarily* direct services or primarily a social change ministry?

3. Is the ministry for which resources are sought one in which the primary emphasis is on hiring someone to carry out the ministry of the church, *or* is it one in which the primary emphasis is on opening new opportunities for laymen and clergymen to respond directly to the call to ministry and service? To which does the organization usually give the higher priority? Is this a criterion?

4. What are the expectations of those seeking resources for future allocations? In coming years, will larger or smaller quantities of resources be sought?

5. Will this allocation increase the capability of the organi-

zation to carry out its mission without additional financial assistance in the future?

6. Is there an evangelistic thrust to this ministry?

7. What are the lines of accountability that are present or proposed, and to whom is this ministry accountable? How? How do the lines of accountability run to (*a*) the clientele, (*b*) the policy-makers, (*c*) the source of funds?

8. As the definition of purpose or need changes, who decides which new programs should be adopted? Staff? Director? Clientele? Board? Who has the initiative? What are the lines of accountability?

9. If this request for allocation of resources is completely rejected, what will be the probable consequences?

10. If this is a continuing ministry, what has been learned from past experiences about this type of venture? How will next year's program differ from last year's?

11. In terms of total dollar expenditures, how much is allocated for (*a*) identifying new needs, (*b*) responding to those newly identified needs, (*c*) carrying out existing program, (*d*) keeping the organization going (institutional maintenance)?

12. In terms of the specific goals and objectives you set for this ministry at the beginning of this year, what is your progress in reaching them? What are the mileposts being used to measure direction and pace?

13. If you were suddenly given a $15,000 grant for each of the next three years *over and above* your budget request, how would you use it?

14. Which congregations—not ministers—have the closest ties to this venture?

15. What is the closest parallel ministry in your community or city?

16. In performance budgeting terms, what are the unit costs of the *output* of your ministry? For example, does it cost $25 or $40 or $60 for each child placed in a host home through the summer family-exchange program? On an average at-

tendance basis, what is the cost per day of the nursery school at the Community Center? (It is about a dollar per child-hour of attendance at many nursery schools and day care centers —why the difference?) What is the annual cost per family that is served by this ministry?

17. Are any changes in physical facilities contemplated? If yes, what will be the total capital costs of the change? What will be the *annual* impact on the *operating* budget?

18. Should the denomination encourage or require "client representation" at the hearings where budget requests by church-related agencies are presented? Should the presentation be limited only to the producer of the services or include also the consumers of those services?

Perhaps the most significant long-term result of the growing influence of economic considerations on the decision-making processes in the churches will be an increase in the demand for accountability. That also introduces the subject of evaluation and thus merits a separate chapter.

8 Friends, Pastors, Leaders, and Managers

"If I understand the question correctly, you're asking what I see as the most important single change that has occurred here at St. Luke's during the past twenty years," reflected Mrs. Adams, who had joined that parish in 1954. "That's an easy one! During the last twenty years we have had three pastors, Dr. Hanson, Pastor Anderson, and now Ed Jackson."

"I'm not sure I understand your point," was the reply.

"The most important change that has taken place here at St. Luke's during the time I've been a member has been in the changing style of our ministerial leadership," Mrs. Adams went on. "This change in leadership style is reflected by terms we use in referring to or in addressing our pastor. Dr. Hanson had a very strong personality and he ran this parish. He was a very authoritarian *Herr Pastor* type. You either did it the way Dr. Hanson wanted it done or you got out. Occasionally he would ask individual members of the church council privately for their advice, but when my husband, who was on the church council for several years, left the house to go to a council meeting he used to say, 'Well, tonight is the night we go to receive our marching orders for next month.' That's about the way it was, too.

"Dr. Hanson was followed in 1963 by Pastor Anderson, who was just the opposite type. When he graduated from seminary he went to a small parish downstate and while there he did additional graduate work in counseling. He was a wonderful pastor, a pretty fair preacher, and an awfully nice person. But if you asked him what time it was he would ask what time you would like it to be or why you asked. He may have had some good ideas about what St. Luke's should do in response to the critical issues of the 1960s, but if he did, he sure kept them to himself! My husband was elected to the church council again a couple of years after Pastor Anderson came here, but after a year he resigned out of sheer frustration. Every time he came home after the monthly church council meeting he would be so mad he couldn't go to bed for two or three hours. One time he growled that trying to get Pastor Anderson to give direction or take the lead was like trying to nail a custard pie to the wall. I guess it was too much of a change to switch from the dictatorial style of Dr. Hanson to the completely nondirective approach of Pastor Anderson.

"After Pastor Anderson resigned to go into the hospital chaplaincy," continued Mrs. Adams, "we called Ed Jackson. Ed is first of all a wonderful Christian individual. He is a person. Second, he is a warm, understanding and helpful pastor. Third, he knows how to be a leader and is willing to be an active leader. Third, he's a good manager. A parish the size of St. Luke's doesn't need and can't afford a business manager, but it can't run under its own momentum.

"I guess what I'm trying to say," she summarized, "is that Dr. Hanson was the man in charge of St. Luke's. He ran it. We respected him and we treated him with respect, so we called him Doctor Hanson out of respect. We saw our next minister as an overtrained individual who was trying too hard to be the kind of pastor he had been taught to be, so we called him Pastor Anderson. He tried so hard to be a good pastor, and I guess we thought it would help him, or at least make him feel good, if we called him "Pastor," and so that's how we addressed him. Incidentally, he always referred to himself as 'your pastor' or as 'the pastor of this parish' or in some similar manner. When Ed came, he came as a warm, friendly human being, so we all addressed him by his first name. The children and a few of our older members address him as 'Pastor Jackson,' but for 90 percent of the youth, he's 'Ed Jackson,' a very close friend, a warm pastor, a trusted leader, and a competent manager."

After three years with one of the larger national agencies in his denomination, a minister was commenting on the leadership style and competence of the executive director of the agency. " The most influential single factor in my decision to leave the parish ministry and take this job," he reflected, "was the attractive personality of the executive director. I couldn't think of anyone I would rather have living next door to me, and I couldn't imagine how anyone could be a better pastor than this man. I figured if I couldn't be effective under his leadership it would be my fault, not his. We're still great friends and he's still a wonderful guy. But I want out! He is an indecisive leader and he doesn't know even one of the first principles of managing a large organization. Do you know of any parish where I might fit that's open?"

Both of these individuals were emphasizing two of the factors most neglected in improving the decision-making capability of the churches. The first is the distinction between four roles—friend, pastor, leader, and manager. Many people are inclined to assume that the qualities that are found in a good friend and/or the qualities that make a good pastor also make a good leader or administrator.

The second distinction is between the qualities found in an excellent leader and those found in an effective manager. Here again the overlap is less than 100 percent. The leader is primarily concerned with his relationships with people, whereas the manager must also be conscious of the behavior patterns of institutions and organizations.

One indication of a limited recognition of this distinction is that several hundred congregations and a few denominational agencies employ one person to fill the pastor-leader role and another individual to fill the manager or administrator role. The distinction is far more widely recognized in business and government, where thousands of organizations have a politician (pastor)-leader type in the top position and a manager in the number two slot in the organization.

The personal attributes, skills, orientation, and responsibilities of a good manager are not identical with those of a good leader. The contributions of the friendly pastor to the decision-making process often differ significantly from those of the charismatic leader, and these differ from the contributions of the knowledgeable manager.

A somewhat oversimplified example of these differences can be seen in the response to the situation produced when costs rise more rapidly than does income. The pastoral type tends to refer the problem to "those responsible for raising money," while the leader seeks to become directly involved in increasing the income of the organization, and the manager tends to look at both income and expenditures to investigate where and how costs can be reduced.

In other words, one of the factors involved in the response to a question or the demand for a decision is influenced by the primary self-identification of the person who holds a decision-making responsibility. This is not to suggest that no one person can possess the qualifications required for being a good pastor, an influential leader, and an effective manager. Some individuals have a high level of competence in all three roles, but most of us tend to identify more comfortably with one role than with either of the other two. But it is possible for a person to improve his or her skills in any of the areas mentioned here, including the skills necessary for meaningful and creative friendships.

In general, the churches have concentrated on in-service training programs for both the laity and the clergy directed at helping people improve their capability to relate to other people as persons. It is hard to overestimate the good that has been produced by these efforts. It is even more difficult to measure the harm done by the church-sponsored efforts in this area which have been led by incompetent, poorly trained, maladjusted, or overzealous "trainers" and leaders.[1]

This movement has been pioneered in the business world by behavioral scientists who became involved in business administration in the academic community and also functioned as consultants to corporations. Shortly after the end of World War I, following a perspective that interpreted man as an economic creature, other theories won adherents and an operational response in the business world. Elton Mayo called to the attention of the business community the importance of man as a social creature.[2] This challenged the economic man interpretation and marked the beginnings of the serious study of interpersonal relationships in industry.

The next major figure to add a new dimension to the study of leadership and administration in an organization was Kurt Lewin.[3] Lewin and others challenged both the effectiveness of the traditional bureaucratic structure and the concept of unilateral power.

Perhaps the most significant break with the traditional concepts of bureaucracy, leadership styles, and motivation was produced by Douglas McGregor and his X and Y theories.[4] McGregor suggested that the traditional assumption that man had to be forced to work could be described as Theory X. He proposed that a more realistic theory was that man naturally tends to find work meaningful and rewarding if the conditions permit this to happen. He called this Theory Y, and it coincides with the concept of self-actualization.

More recently a far more complex theory of the nature of man has been offered by Elliott Jaques and Harry Levinson.[b] They define psychological man and emphasize the importance of a human being's need to reach his ego ideal.

These models of social man, man as a self-actualizing creature, and man as a complex and developing person interacting with his environment have had a tremendous influence in the business world. They have also had a major impact on leadership training programs for public and private organizations, including the churches.

By the early 1960s, however, business leaders had begun to

question the training programs that had been built on the assumption that a happier and more productive worker could be produced by improving the employee's ability to relate to other people. As one businessman explained, "We sent scores of our people to sensitivity training. With about half of them nothing happened and so no harm was done. But some of our most valued employees came back as radically changed persons. The sensitivity training had greatly improved their ability to understand themselves and to relate to our people; but they came back to the same old slot in the same old organization. Before long they were so discontented they quit. Finally we realized that what we were doing was paying to train some of our best employees to quit. So we dropped the sensitivity training and have been concentrating on changing our organization rather than our people."

This man was describing a change which has only just begun to be felt in the churches, namely, the shift from an emphasis on training in interpersonal relationships to an emphasis on *both* these experiences *and* on changing the organization.[6]

What does all this have to do with how decisions are made in the churches?

There are at least four lessons that stand out from the discussion thus far. First, there is a difference in the influences brought to the decision-making table between the leader who thinks primarily in terms of interpersonal relationships and the manager who thinks primarily in terms of how organizations and institutions function. Second, the individual who is "a great guy" or "a wonderful friend" may or may not be a good leader or an effective administrator. Third, helping people improve their ability to understand themselves and to relate to others may not improve the operation or effectiveness of an organization.[7] Finally, the perspective of the leader or manager is influenced by his frame of reference. As the pastor, the leader, or the manager seeks to influence the behavior of others, to arouse a response from people or to affect the operation of an organization or institution, the methods or techniques he uses will be determined by his perspective, assumptions, and frame of reference.

Perspectives and Methods

Though he may not be consciously and systematically aware of it, every leader's style is derived from his view of the nature of man. This basic point can be illustrated by looking at the subject from two different perspectives. The first is described by this diagram.[8]

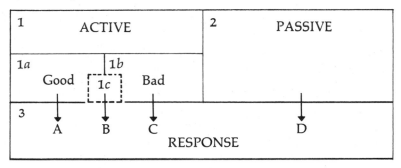

The first division is between (1) the leader who sees most people as active, self-actualizing, and self-motivating individuals who can generate their own ideas and make their own decisions and (2) the leader who sees people as passive creatures responding to their environment and external stimuli but unable to motivate themselves. The first reflects the view of Lewin, McGregor, and others. The second reflects the views of such influential men as the political philosopher John Locke and the psychologist B. F. Skinner.

The second division is a subdivision of the leaders in the first category. This division is between (1a) the leader who sees people as good and operates on the assumption that if the institutional, social, political, and economic barriers can be lowered people will do what is right and good and (1b) the leader who acts on the assumption that people are bad and unless man is restrained he will hurt both his neighbor and himself. The Christian doctrine of man is based on the paradox that man is good (created in God's image) and bad (the Fall). Therefore the Christian view is represented by the box (1c) enclosed with a dotted line in this diagram.

The style or methods of every leader are reflected by one of the four vertical arrows in the diagram. The leader who assumes that man is an active creature who wants to do good will follow a style represented by arrow A. In exercising his leadership role in regard to the responses of people this type of leader will direct his efforts largely at identifying and removing the barriers that keep his self-motivated or self-actualizing people from doing good. This leader or administrator will probably find useful Frederick Herzberg's contributions on the critical importance of meaningful work that provides a direct feedback of self-satisfactions. [9]

The style of the leader who shares the belief that man is an active creature, but who differs at the next point by believing that man is inherently bad, will direct his leadership at identifying the points of action where man is most likely to hurt his neighbor and himself. This leader's energies will be devoted to creating barriers around people to keep them from hurting both themselves and others. His style, actions, and methods in regard to how people respond in any situation are represented by arrow C. This leader will devote a large amount of time and energy to securing the adoption of rules, regulations, and laws which prohibit certain actions and activities by people and which require conformity to a precisely defined code of conduct. He will find Machiavelli's *The Prince* filled with what he perceives as helpful and relevant insights.[10]

The leader who believes that man is both good and bad will develop a style represented by arrow B. At times he will devote his time and talents to increasing the freedom of people, and at other times he will devote his energies to restricting the freedom of man. This leader, for example, may support the general concept of legalized abortion but oppose permitting abortions to be performed except in licensed facilities by licensed persons. Or a leader holding this doctrine of man may oppose abortions except in cases of rape and incest or where the health or life of the mother is endangered.

The leader who is convinced that B. F. Skinner[11] is right, and those who agree that man's behavior can be shaped by environmental and psychological conditioning, will adopt the methods appropriate to that set of assumptions. Since man's behavior is shaped by external or outside forces the appropriate methods are punishment and reward, or positive and negative "reinforcements." These have been symbolized by the carrot and the stick so often that this approach to management has been described as "the great jackass fallacy." [12]

Who's in Charge Here?

Another perspective for examining how a leader's frame of reference influences his choice of methods, procedures, and techniques in administration can be found in four sets of answers to the question "Who's in charge here?"

The varying responses to this question reveal one of the most serious divisions in the churches—a division that ignores denominational and polity lines.

The responses to this question also reveal one of the two or three most influential forces in the decision-making processes of the churches.

The responses to this question will have a major impact on the dropout rate among ministers, the role of the laity in the church, the life expectancy of thousands of congregations, the level of giving in the churches, the lay-clergy gap, the growing division between young ministers and older clergymen, potential schisms within several of the larger Protestant denominations, and the training of the next generation of clergymen.

The responses to this question constitute the most important single issue in the implementation of the various "restructure" proposals that have been adopted by several denominations.

The responses to this question are already sharply increasing the anxiety level among some ministers and reducing it among others—regardless of which answer is offered in a specific situation.

1. "Who's in charge here?"

When the most frequent response to that question is the name of an individual or the title of an office, this usually means that the leadership style reflects what is still the most common pattern in American organizational life.

The dominant leadership style in most American organizations today, including the churches, is the traditional one. It is an hierarchical style, with the highest authority figure at the top of the pyramid. It is the style most familiar to anyone over thirty, to veterans of World War II and the Korean War, to anyone who has worked in a large organization, either public or private, and to anyone who has had the traditional form of management training.

It is the style encountered most frequently in the local church where the pastor is usually either sitting in the top seat in the pyramid or at least is assumed to be occupying that position. (In real life the top seat in the seldom seen power pyramid in a local church may be occupied by an elderly layman, while the pastor is in the top seat in the ceremonial pyramid that is on public display. If the pastor is aware of the existence of the other pyramid, this may be a source of considerable anxiety to him.)

This hierarchical style of ministerial leadership is viewed by many as normative in the local church and can be illustrated both by the *Herr Pastor* model in the German Lutheran congregation and by the suggestion that one clergyman be designated to serve as chief executive officer of the parish in the proposed, but now deceased, plan of church union that emerged out of the Consultation on Church Union.

Hierarchical leadership is almost universal in denominational and interdenominational structures. Here the top seat in the pyramid is occupied by someone with a title such as bishop, president, executive secretary, stated clerk, director, dean, rector, moderator, minister, or chairman. This long and varied list of titles is not as confusing as it may at first appear. At the end of the first six weeks, the typical first-grader knows the redbirds are the fast readers and the bluebirds are the slow readers. Churchmen see through labels almost as quickly as first-graders.

The significance of titles should not be underestimated, however. Titles can often be used to reinforce the hierarchical style of leadership. The minister who is elected to the office that carries with it the title "Bishop" usually finds it more difficult to avoid the authoritarian dimensions of hierarchical structure than does the man who is elected to an office that bears the title "Executive Secretary" or "Minister" or "President."

Likewise, in the local church, people who are comfortable with the hierarchical style of parish leadership are usually more comfortable with a title such as "Reverend" or "Doctor" for the pastor than with the growing pattern of addressing the pastor by his first name.

The hierarchical leadership structure is under a most vigorous attack in the churches today. Occasionally this is an affirmative attack, such as that of Gerald Jud when he refers to the problems created by the "Big Daddy fantasy" [13] in the local churches, or the direct frontal attack that has been launched by hundreds of young priests in the Roman Catholic Church. The hierarchical structure is under attack by many young ministers, both Protestant and Catholic, who are not interested in the "Big Daddy" role and strongly prefer to be a part of a team ministry.

It is also under scattered attack by a few individuals who are still opposing some of the recently adopted proposals for denominational restructuring on the grounds that the restructuring proposal perpetuated and reinforced the existing hierarchical style or, even worse in the eyes of these critics, ignored the subject altogether.

Within the churches the most threatening attack on the

hierarchical style of organizational leadership is coming from a growing number of laymen and a few ministers who are simply saying, "No, thanks," and walking away from the organization. This response can be seen in the action of many priests who are leaving the professional ministry of the Roman Catholic Church, in the withholding of funds by laymen of various faiths, in the attitude of thousands of young people toward the church, and in the tremendous apathy aroused by the *Plan of Union* of the Consultation on Church Union, which was viewed by many as simply producing a larger pyramid filled with many smaller pyramids.

Outside the churches the hierarchical style of organizational leadership is under very serious attack in the armed forces and in scores of universities, colleges, and theological seminaries. It is already on its deathbed in the family. As was pointed out earlier, the most constructive attack was launched in the business community in the 1950s and led by a new band of scholars in management who had been trained in the behavioral sciences.

One of the pioneers in this attack, and one of the most creative proponents of a new style of organizational leadership, the late Douglas McGregor, wrote in 1950, "Out of all this has come the first clear recognition of an inescapable fact: we cannot successfully *force* people to work for management's objectives. The ancient conception that people will do the work of the world only if they are forced to do so by threats or intimidation, or by the camouflaged authoritarian methods of paternalism, has been suffering from a lingering fatal illness for a quarter of a century. I venture the guess that it will be dead in another decade." [14]

While McGregor was unduly optimistic in his prediction (it normally takes at least one full generation to substantially change a long-established behavior pattern), he was absolutely correct in predicting a new life-style and a new set of values which would require the evaluation of a new form of organizational life.

The response to this demand for a new style of organizational leadership is most visible in the business world. In one recent year, for example, *Fortune* carried a dozen major articles which dealt either directly or indirectly with this issue.

The hierarchical style of organizational leadership also has its defenders. It is defended (naturally) by many, but not all, of those who sit in the seat at the top of one of the pyramids. It is being defended by those who argue that this is what people are used to, what they accept, and, therefore, it is what they like and what is good for them. It is being defended by pragmatists who contend that to simply knock down the pyramid would lead to chaos, and therefore it must be perpetuated until a better form or style is developed and can be implemented.

2. "Who's in charge here?" "They are."

This response is usually made in a tone of voice that ranges from neutral to apathetic to hostile, except on those occasions when "they" have committed a highly visible error and it is clear that "they" will have to suffer publicly the consequences of their action.

Nearly all churches are organized, both congregationally and denominationally, on the principle of representative government. Although some, such as the Southern Baptist Convention, send "messengers" rather than "delegates" to national conventions in order to avoid seeming to delegate authority to a few who represent the many, relatively few small congregations actually function on the basis of participatory democracy. In several denominations, such as the Presbyterians and Episcopalians, a very large grant of authority is given to a small central governing board. Thus the 20-member session of an 800-member Presbyterian congregation may decide to drastically alter the program or double the budget or remodel the meeting place or revise the Sunday morning schedule without asking the opinion of the members or seeking their approval. While this system has the advantage of pinpointing responsibility and expediting action, the price tag on this advantage is the lack of a broad base of participation in the decision-making process. This means that the Presbyterian session, or the vestry in an Episcopal parish, may approve an action which few of the members are interested in helping to implement.

Likewise the 16-member vestry in an 800-member Episcopalian church may call a new rector and simply announce this fact to the congregation. The members do not have a voice in the selection of their new pastor. It is easy for members not in leadership positions to respond to such critical decisions by this small but powerful governing body with the words "Well, they made the decision let them implement it."

One of the most urgent and most important challenges to the leaders in the churches today is how to reduce the widening "we-they" gap. This gap is a product of the structure of the decision-making process which causes those not directly involved in making decisions to respond to the question "Who's in charge here?" with a shrug and the words "They are."

This gap is far less significant in congregations where the opportunities to build the trust level are comparatively numerous than it is within denominational families where the advertising phrase "Never trust a stranger" appears to be a guideline in the people's attitudes toward denominational decision-making structures.

3. "Who's in charge here?" "Golly, now that you raise the question, I guess the answer is no one."

This response reflects a third style of organizational leadership. It is most often found in the organization that for years has been governed through the traditional hierarchical pyramid, often with an authoritarian personality in the top seat, and now has a new leader who has chosen to be nondirective in his leadership style and who rejects both the hierarchical pyramid and the authoritarian role.

The result is often inaction, and may reach the point of

chaos. Decisions are made by indecision. A choice among several alternative courses of action is often made by allowing all viable options except one to expire. Expectations are seldom articulated (that would be too authoritarian), and if they are stated, are rarely phrased in meaningful operational terms. There is a tendency to neglect basic organizational procedures such as the use of written messages as a follow-up on informal conversations, management by objective, and cost accounting.

The sudden introduction of this nondirective style of organizational leadership in a local church often means that the institution is paralyzed, the lay leadership is frustrated, and the congregation is immobilized in the face of change.

In a denominational or interdenominational organization, the replacement of the traditional hierarchical pyramid with this style of nondirective leadership often means that many programs are proposed, but few are implemented; goals are articulated, but seldom fulfilled; there is a restlessness among the clientele, and the financial receipts tend to decline.

In several respects this style of leadership is the most destructive of any described here to *both* the institution and the people.

4. "Who's in charge here?" "We all are."

This response reflects a fourth style of organizational leadership—a style that promises to become the dominant style of the 1970s in the churches, as it already has in several other segments of American society.

In this style of organizational leadership, greater emphasis in motivating the participants is placed on such factors as mutual trust, participation in the formulation of the organization's goals and objectives, self-direction, personal growth, and a climate of openness. Traditional motivational factors, such as organizational loyalty, precedent, coercion, seniority, and authority of position, are either cast aside completely or largely ignored. Knowledge rather than position, competence rather than seniority, trust rather than authority, self-expression rather than conformity, and adaptation rather than precedent, emerge as the characteristics of the organization with this style of leadership.

A number of different labels have been applied to this style of organizational leadership. The list includes team management, collaborative, participatory, democratic, and shared leadership.

The administrative processes accompanying this style of leadership usually leave much to be desired. Often conspicuous by their absence are such standard administrative procedures as screening alternatives by considering the probable consequences or implications of each one, making action decisions only after attaining the necessary degree of commitment by those responsible for implementing and/or living with the consequences of that decision, reliable internal communication, and the development *in advance* of the criteria to be used in evaluation.

Gradually, however, an increasing number of people are developing the skills necessary to improve the effectiveness of this style of leadership, and thus also the psychi rewards to the participants in this pattern of decision-making. Once they have seen "Paree" it is hard to keep them down on the farm.

Evaluating and Choosing Leaders

In a recent evaluation of the performance of college teachers of calculus two criteria were developed. One was subjective. This was stated in the question asked each student at the end of the course: "What grade would you assign to your instructor's total teaching performance?" The grades of the students taught by each instructor were averaged, and that average became the grade assigned to that instructor. The other measurement was objective. Each student was tested in an exceptionally thorough manner to determine how much he or she had learned in terms of the content of the course. (Calculus was selected because it is a content course in which the content learned can be measured.) Each student was graded, and the average of the grades of the students taught by each instructor became the second grade given that instructor. In other words, each instructor received two grades, one based on his students' evaluation of his teaching and the other on how much his students had learned.

The instructors receiving the three lowest grades in the evaluation by the students were the three receiving the highest grades on the basis of what the students had learned. The instructor ranking highest in the evaluation by his students ranked lowest on the objective test of how much his students had learned. For the entire group of instructors the correlation between student performance and student evaluation was —.746.[15]

The results of this experiment suggest three questions that may be appropriate for consideration by persons seeking to evaluate or to choose leaders: (1) What are the qualities desired in the leader? (2) Does the evaluation instrument measure these qualities? (3) Are there any probable incompatibilities between the desired qualities?

The most widespread and frequently recognized illustration of the third of these questions is the desire in many ecclesiastical organizations to find a leader who is both an effective pastor and an excellent administrator. Very rarely are both of these qualities combined in the same person. This introduces the concept of "trade-off" into the evaluation and selection process. How much of one desired quality can be "traded off" in order to secure a minimum level of competence in the other quality?

Leadership Qualities

When this distinction between friends, pastors, leaders, and managers is used to distinguish between the participants in the ecclesiastical decision-making process, it provides a frame of reference for reviewing some of the qualities most desirable in the person chosen as the leader and/or manager in a religious organization. It cannot be emphasized too strongly that these qualities will not necessarily be found in a person's best friend or in the outstanding pastor.

1. Leaders do lead. By definition the essential quality of leadership is leadership. For a quarter of a century following World War II many theological seminaries taught courses in nondirective counseling, partly on the premise that the incompetent counselor would probably do less harm utilizing this style than with a more directive approach. Unfortunately some students in these courses apparently thought they were taking courses in church administration. One result is a large number of clergy who have developed a "nondirective" style of leadership.

An outstanding national illustration of the emergence of the expectation that leaders should lead can be found in the city manager profession. For decades the ethics of the profession decreed that a city manager stayed out of "politics" and simply carried out the policy directives of the city council. His position was defined as an "administrator," not as a leader. After many years of debate, and scores of frustrating experiences in which city managers were dismissed because of their failure to accept the responsibility of leadership, the International City Managers Association revised the role definition to include the concept of "community leader." When for reasons of economy and/or expertise (see item 4 below) a city council decides to delegate authority to the manager, he is expected to accept that delegation of authority. He is hired to be a leader and he is expected to lead.

2. An effective leader or manager recognizes that supervision is always relational.[16] He also recognizes that some leadership styles can be very destructive of people and of relationships, while other styles and factors strengthen and reinforce relationships.

The most destructive style of leadership is no leadership. A close second is the unpredictable, unreliable, inconsistent, and uncertain style which swings like a pendulum from dictatorial to indecisive. A distant third in destructiveness is the consistently autocratic style. Thus the autocratic leader who is consistently autocratic may be disruptive in some situations and constructive in others. The least destructive style is the one which is predictable, is consistent with the expectations of the people in a given situation, encourages meaningful participation, and enables all the participants to develop a sense of shared goals.

3. As this second point suggests, the effective leader is conscious of the situation in which he is functioning and of the expectations generated by that situation. At times the situation may call for the leader to take decisive action unilaterally, and at other times in other situations the effective leader may be considered by some persons to be moving too slowly as he trades off time in order to broaden the base of participation and the ownership of goals.

4. The effective leader recognizes that the reasons why people are willing to delegate authority to others are changing, and that these reasons also vary from time to time. Such traditional sources of authority as position, title, rules, precedent, and custom are diminishing in importance. Increasingly people are willing to delegate authority to one person or to a small group in (*a*) a time of perceived crisis, (*b*) when the person or group holding the delegated authority acts in a manner consistent with the wishes of those delegating authority, (*c*) when knowledge or expertise is accepted as a decisive factor in making decisions, and (*d*) when in the interests of economy of time, money, and energy it is preferable to delegate than to assemble everyone for a democratic decision-making process (few parishes are able to hold five congregational meetings week after week).[17] The effective leader is able to recognize the shifting weight of these four factors from situation to situation.

5. The effective leader is always conscious of the importance of the "compensation" expected by people and of the compensation actually being received by persons in the organization.

This includes not only economic compensation, but also status, appreciation, and a wide range of psychi rewards.[18]

6. The effective leader has many roles, and he recognizes the differences between these roles and knows which one he is being expected to fill at a given time in a given situation.[19] For example, the pastor has the role of conservator of the orthodox Christian faith, and he should be able to fulfill that leadership role when it is expected of him. Likewise the denominational leader counseling with churches should be able to distinguish between his role as (a) a diagnostician when the congregational leaders grant him authority, on the basis of experience, knowledge, and objectivity, to diagnose their problem and (b) a process consultant helping them to understand the nature of the problem and to select a course of action which they will implement (therefore, they have to own that decision).

7. The effective leader listens. There is substantial evidence to suggest that leaders in any organization talk to other leaders, although there is substantially less evidence to suggest that leaders listen to other leaders, and very little evidence to suggest that leaders listen to nonleaders.

The effective leader who takes the expectations of people seriously (see points 2 and 3 above) recognizes the value of listening in discovering and identifying those expectations.

8. The effective ecclesiastical leader recognizes that there are occasions when he is expected to be a prophetic leader. One of the automatic trade-offs on these occasions is widespread popularity. Two outstanding examples of leaders accepting and fulfilling prophetic roles are Walker Knight and Foy Valentine of the Southern Baptist Convention. Knight, as editor of *Home Missions,* and Valentine as executive secretary of the Christian Life Commission, have moved the Southern Baptist Convention further into the last third of the twentieth century than was desired by many Baptists. They have paid a price for their actions, but they have been faithful to their call to prophetic leadership.

9. The effective leader knows where the boundaries are, but he is not always restricted by those boundaries. In his discussion of Presidential leadership Theodore C. Sorensen describes "the outer limits of decision." He suggests that a President always functions within the ever-present limitations of permissibility, resources, time, previous commitments, and available information. [20] The same basic point has been made in somewhat more picturesque language by Thomas Sheppard, who quotes the suggestion of John DeCelles that a leader never gets between the dog and the lamp post.[21] In both cases the point is made that a leader is aware of the limitations which, if violated, tend to produce results that are counterproductive.

The other side of this point is that the effective leader knows when and how these limits or boundaries can be pushed back in order to be made less restrictive. Again Foy Valentine and Walker Knight are examples of practitioners of this skill.

10. Perhaps most important of all, the effective ecclesiastical leader knows when it is time to move on to a new assignment. He knows this for himself, and he is able to recognize it for others.

The number of times when the leader of a religious organization has remained too long in one place greatly exceeds the number of times when a leader has moved prematurely. This generalization can be illustrated by thousands of examples —by lay leaders in the local church, by parish pastors, and by denominational leaders. The tendency to remain too long is more pervasive and more damaging to both the persons involved and the organization than the tendency to move too soon. Staying a year (or a decade) too long is usually more destructive than leaving a year too soon.

In recent years a growing response to this issue has been to promote leadership training, which has proved far less effective than expected.[22] The critical strategy in evaluating and choosing leadership in the churches may not consist in devising instruments of evaluation nor in developing leadership training programs. More likely it consists in moving leaders when the times and the situation suggest a change is appropriate, and in matching the appropriate leader to a particular situation. That is one reason why the responsibilities of bishops, district and synod presidents, district superintendents, conference and regional ministers, and other denominational leaders have moved increasingly toward a specialization in personnel management.

In reviewing these ten qualities of leadership it may be helpful to lift up three generalizations. First, this is not offered as an exhaustive list, but only to suggest that in the churches more is known than practiced about the qualities of leadership. Second, this list of qualities can be expanded and used as a checklist in choosing and evaluating leaders. It will often be more helpful in such efforts than job descriptions, which frequently are so inclusive as to be counterproductive. Third, this list, like other similar lists, should not be taken too seriously. Two recent books in the field of management sciences offer a balancing point of view. In both cases the titles are as suggestive as the contents are enlightening. [23]

Motivation or Manipulation?

"Back when we had only 80 members we used to average 60 at worship on Sunday morning," commented a layman to his pastor one evening. "Now we have nearly 500 members and seldom do we have more than 200 in church on Sunday morning. That means our ratio of attendance-to-membership has dropped from 75 percent to 40 percent."

To cut a long story short, this sixty-five-year-old congregation had suddenly changed from a rural to an exurban parish in the space of five years. As the membership grew, church attendance increased at a slower rate. After discussing this, the leaders decided that each week a team of ten persons with a rotating membership would telephone, visit, or send a note to each member who had been absent that Sunday. The basic content of the message was simply to say, "We missed you."

Immediately attendance began to climb, and after several weeks leveled off at slightly over 300.

Was this manipulation? Or was it motivation? The intention was to let people know they were missed whenever they were absent from corporate worship. The hope was that this would influence behavior patterns. The persons doing this thought it might motivate people to attend more frequently if they knew they were missed whenever they were absent. While it is impossible to absolutely prove a cause and effect relationship, the results were rewarding to those responsible for this venture.

If it is defined as manipulation, had this same congregation been "manipulating" members when they failed to make sure that everyone absent from Sunday morning worship knew he was missed? Had they been manipulating people by allowing the absent members to assume they were not missed? Can manipulation be either overt or covert?

This is an issue that every effective leader must respond to in some manner. Is the Presbyterian minister manipulating the ruling elders when he moves the meeting of the session from a depressing basement fellowship hall to the attractive first-floor church parlor? The attendance percentage jumps from 50 to 80 percent immediately after this change, so it appears that he is influencing behavior patterns. Or is it more accurate to describe him as an intelligent leader and effective manager of a religious organization?

One minister has these two quotations in a prominent place below the glass top on his desk: "A person's loyalty is a function of how much he feels he is appreciated." "The effectiveness of any program depends upon the amount of participation delegated." [24] Are these guidelines to the manipulation of people, or to effective leadership of a complex organization?

Levinson contends that "the most powerful motivating force for any human being is his wish to attain his ego ideal." [25] Is the leader who accepts and operates on this principle motivating or manipulating people?

With regard to these and related questions confronting today's leader, it may be that the most neglected issue is one which has been overlooked in the rush to encourage participation, equalize power, enhance trust, and improve interpersonal relationships. Though each of these management goals is commendable and remarkable progress has been made in the past decade in moving toward these goals, in the process one very important consideration in the decision-making structures of the churches has been overlooked. It is a point on which Douglas McGregor was steadfast, namely, the accountability and responsibility of the organization's appointed or elected leadership.[26] The churches may have neglected this leadership responsibility more than most organizations in American society. Recently, however, perhaps because of financial pressures, the twin issues of evaluation and accountability have begun to receive the attention in the churches which they have long deserved.

9 Evaluation and Accountability

"People simply aren't interested in the church in the same way they were in the 1950s," explained a pastor who had been in the same parish for twenty-five years. "In the middle fifties we used to average over 300 at worship on Sunday morning. Now we're delighted when attendance goes over the 200 mark."

卐

"The churches aren't interested in social action or in helping others the way they used to be," remarked a United Presbyterian denominational executive. "In our denomination the giving by the churches for General Assembly causes has dropped by a third. If Presbyterians really were concerned about others, our receipts for General Assembly causes would be increasing rather than decreasing."

卐

"The General Conference spoke a lot of pious words in Atlanta about 'emerging social issues,' but it's obvious no one in The United Methodist Church really is very much concerned about social action," complained a member of the Board of Church and Society. "If the General Conference had really been interested in having the church deal with emerging social issues they would have provided additional funding for our agency."

卐

"The denominations are playing games with ecumenicity," commented the executive of a small interdenominational agency, with bitterness in his voice. "In the face of inflation and rising costs our income from the denominations has dropped 10 percent during the past three years. Why don't they just come out openly and say they aren't interested in ecumenicity any longer?"

🙾

"The university student is the 'nigger' of the 1970s," declared a clergyman for an interdenominational university campus ministry. "There used to be five ministers on the staff of this center; now there are three, and we have barely enough income from the churches to support the three of us. Don't tell me the people in the churches are interested in a ministry to students!"

🙾

The five sets of comments above reflect two of the most serious deficiencies in the decision-making processes of the churches. These are the closely related subjects of an inadequate system of evaluation and a third-rate system of accountability.

In each of the incidents the person quoted is offering an evaluation statement. The pastor has evaluated and is reporting on his evaluation of a decline in interest by people in the corporate worship services in his parish. The United Presbyterian leader is offering an evaluation of Presbyterians' interest in outreach and social action. The disgruntled Methodist is evaluating his denomination's real concern over emerging social issues. The campus minister is evaluating the churches' interest in a ministry to students.

Compare these "evaluations" with this statement by the manager of a supermarket: "It's obvious that people aren't interested in spending money on food or in shopping in large stores. Our volume has dropped 12 percent since I became the manager of this store two years ago." It is possible that a more precise description of the situation would be that people are still buying food and still prefer the large supermarkets, but they may not be as interested as they formerly were in shopping at that particular store under the current manager.

Hundreds of congregations and at least a half dozen of the

larger denominations are in financial difficulty because of the lack of an adequate system of accountability. These denominations are large bureaucracies serving a largely captive clientele. Despite the highly visible exceptions, it appears that, in fact, few church members feel free to leave their denomination. [1] If they are bored or unhappy with their parish or their denomination, many apparently feel they have no alternative but to "drop out." In many communities they do have the freedom to transfer their membership to another congregation of the same denomination, but in most communities their congregation holds the only franchise granted by that denomination. They have only a very limited understanding of the purpose or goals of their congregation, and even less awareness of the total program and ministry of their denomination. The *Reader's Digest* has ten times as many readers as all the denominational periodicals combined. The typical church member has neither the time nor the resources to make an evaluation of what his church is doing. Furthermore, if he does feel unhappy with what is happening he cannot express his discontent in the election booth as he does when he is unhappy about the performance of the President of the United States, or the mayor of his city, or a senator.

Perhaps the most widely known illustration of the tendency of the unhappy church member to express his discontent by withholding funds or "dropping out" came after the $10,000 grant to the Angela Davis Defense Fund by an agency of The United Presbyterian Church. Though an unprecedented number of congregations and presbyteries communicated their discontent by writing letters and sending formal expressions of protest, many Presbyterians felt very frustrated over their inability to register a stronger protest.

Which System of Accountability?

It would be easy to jump from this discussion to the conclusion that the churches lack any system of accountability. *That is not true!*

A more accurate statement would be to say that the churches have a very poor system of accountability.

In analyzing the alternatives for improving the effectiveness of the various systems providing social services to people, such as education and health care, Alice M. Rivlin has suggested three models for improving the relationship between the producers of social services and the consumers. One is decentralization, a second is community control, and a third is the marketplace.[2]

Although she developed this model of accountability to provide a frame of reference for improving effectiveness in delivering social services, it is also a useful frame of reference for examining the system of accountability in the decision-making processes of the churches.

The illustrations used earlier in this chapter all suggest the use of a limited marketplace model of accountability. This means that if the consumer is dissatisfied he may go elsewhere to shop for the same services. The model used by the churches, however, is a very inadequate model of the marketplace concept for three major reasons.

First, the monopolistic nature of the churches' operations usually means that the marketplace model is not operative. Relatively few Presbyterians or Episcopalians or Lutherans have another church of their own denomination as convenient to them as the one to which they belong. Relatively few congregations are free to switch denominational labels on their building if they are dissatisfied with the policies, programs, or leadership of their denomination. Relatively few denominations which have committed themselves to an ecumenical approach in a ministry to university students are really free to drop out of that arrangement and put their dollars into a different arrangement on that same campus. Relatively few denominational program agencies are free to switch to another "sponsor" if they become dissatisfied with the support they receive from their own denomination. Relatively few denominations feel free to switch to another program agency if they become dissatisfied with the quality of services they receive from one of their program boards.

In other words, the marketplace model of accountability is about as operative in the churches as it is for the typical homeowner as he looks at his telephone service or the operation of the gas company and the electric utility that supply these services to his home. Either he can take what they deliver or he can discontinue use of that service. Complaints to the regulatory authority are the only alternative, but seldom do these produce satisfactory responses.

A second limitation on the marketplace model as a method of accountability in the churches is that both "producers" and "consumers" encourage brand name loyalty. This greatly reduces the freedom of choice, which is the essential characteristic of the marketplace if it is to be the basic means of accountability. The Presbyterian contemplating a switch from his own church finds himself equally uncomfortable with the red hymnbook at the Lutheran church down the street and the new green book at the Episcopal church on the corner. (It must be added that more than a few Episcopalians are also uncomfortable with the trial liturgy, but their loyalty to the brand name has usually been sufficient to offset that discomfort.)

The third limitation on the marketplace model of accountability is that in theory it runs counter to the concept of a Christian church as a congregation of the followers of Jesus Christ who accept the discipline that goes with the commitment to Christ and the vows of church membership. By definition the church member is not as free to change churches as he is to change dentists or supermarkets or breakfast cereals.

What are the alternatives?

Rivlin's conceptual model suggests two.

One is decentralization—a policy already a part of the structure of such denominations as the Mennonite Church and The Lutheran Church–Missouri Synod, and the choice of the recently restructured United Presbyterian Church. De-centralization as a means of countering the lack of accountability inherent in any large bureaucracy has traditionally been a position advocated by conservatives, but in recent years an increasing number of liberals have begun to have serious doubts about the validity of centralism.[3] Translated into ecclesiastical terms this approach suggests that certain functions —pensions for example—should be centralized, but the creation and administration of highly specialized urban ministries should be decentralized.

Rivlin's second alternative, community control, is the one being chosen by an increasing number of congregations. Translated into churchy terms this means that more and more congregations are selecting their own "mission" projects and allocating a larger share of their benevolence giving directly to these rather than sending those dollars to a regional or national denominational agency to be allocated for mission projects. It is presumed that since these local projects are closer to the people who are financing them than are those whose financing is done through a central headquarters agency, there will be improved accountability to the sources of financing. This is a somewhat precarious view. An examination of actual practices suggests that tradition and public relations, rather than improved accountability, are important factors in the actual allocation of funds.

Another Alternative

Perhaps the best approach to improved accountability in the churches is to improve the quality of the evaluation processes. In recent years the most serious questions about both accountability and the quality of the ministry have been directed at the interdenominational or interfaith ministries on the university campus. This offers a good example for looking at both evaluation and accountability.

To whom are the staff members accountable? To the students? To the administration? To an advisory board? To the denominations funding this ministry? To the church members who believe they are helping finance a ministry to students? To each other? To the faculty? To the pastors of nearby churches? To those congregations meeting on or near the campus?

The simplest system of accountability is one in which the sources of funding, the clientele, and the policy-makers are all represented in one group. Who sets policy for the cooperative campus ministry? Who constitutes the clientele? Who should be the primary source of funding?

These are all structural questions, and though they are basic to any improvement in the quality of the system of accountability, they have limited relevance when discussed in isolation.

The other half of the discussion concerns the substance or content of the accountability system. This is where some form of evaluation is required. What are the standards or the criteria for evaluation of the cooperative ministry? Without regard to lines of accountability, what is the content of the evaluation? Should the evaluation be in the context of the original purpose of the campus ministry? Or should the evaluation be directed at what the staff members are doing in ministry? (The purpose and product of an organization are often not the same thing. See page 66.) Or should the evaluation be based on the needs of the client? If so, who is the client? The individual student? The student who is alienated from the traditional institutional expressions of the church? The university? The faculty? The structures and systems of that social institution described as "higher education"?

Or should the evaluation of this campus ministry focus on how the resources (time, energy, money, physical facilities, materials, etc.) are allocated? If so, should this emphasize the priorities for the allocation of resources? Or should it emphasize the *process* for ordering these priorities?

Finally, it must be asked, why is this evaluation being carried out and who is the client for the product of this evaluation? Is it a part of the established system of accountability?

Is it for determining future allocations of money and manpower? Is it in response to a recently perceived crisis?

Only when these and similar questions have received carefully thought-out and organizationally responsible answers will it be possible to produce a meaningful evaluation of the typical cooperative ministry on the large university campus. Only when there is a meaningful format for the evaluation process will it be possible to improve the system of accountability of the cooperative campus ministry.

This same basic outline can be transferred to a discussion of the accountability of denominational agencies[4] and to a discussion of the accountability and evaluation systems in individual congregations.[5]

All across American society there is a new ground swell of interest in quality, performance, productivity, and excellence. Inevitably similar pressures will be felt in decision-making circles of the churches. As this happens there will be a mounting demand for better systems of accountability and for more meaningful methods of evaluation. In addition to these pressures, the traditional reliance on a marketplace model of evaluation and accountability is forcing a serious reconsideration of that concept. These pressures mean that the marketplace model will either have to be greatly improved (see pages 150-67) or discarded and replaced by new structures of accountability and new efforts to improve both the format and the content of the evaluation process. As this happens it will produce major improvements in the decision-making processes of the churches!

10 The Context for Tomorrow

"When all the facets of M.P.M. (Market Place Ministries) are fully operational at Landmark, we will be in an ecumenical ministry of a dimension that is unprecedented. In all probability, we will be 'landmarking' a movement in Christianity that will be extended beyond our imagination. . . . While Market Place Ministries is a unique expression of the mission of the church it is to be financially self-supporting. . . . It is conceivable that this may be a turn in the road of Church history in our times. . . . M.P.M. is like putting an additional four lanes on an existing four lane highway of the Church's mission. That superhighway leads beyond our present capacity to imagine the implications of M.P.M." (Excerpted from the prospectus for Market Place Ministries dated December 6, 1967, and February 23, 1968.)

Four years later a report evaluating this venture noted that "Market Place Ministries failed, at a tremendous cost to the Church." The huge capital costs and the consistent operating losses forced it to close after the first year of operation.

When prisoners seized control of the Attica Correctional Facility in September, 1971, they held a number of guards as hostages and threatened to cut the throats of the hostages if any attempt was made to retake the prison by force. On the morning of Monday, September 13, the New York State Police and a group of correction officers recaptured control of the prison. The lead article in the *New York Times* on Tuesday morning, September 14, stated that "several of the hostages—prison guards and civilian workers—died when convicts slashed their throats with knives . . . five were killed instantaneously by the inmates."

A few days later it was learned that nine hostages had been

killed (one died four weeks later) and all ten died of gunshot wounds, probably from bullets fired by their rescuers. None had had their throats cut.[1]

There are nearly a dozen churches across the country that boast of operating the world's largest Sunday School.

In 1957 a Lutheran parish began to plan for the construction of a housing project for the elderly on land near the church building. Seven years later the parish had invested a total of $85,000 in "seed money" in the venture with the expectation that most of this would be returned to the parish after completion of the project. When the project was completed in 1966 at a cost of $2.7 million the parish had an investment of $418,000 in the form of a forty-year no-interest "loan."

These incidents illustrate what for an increasing number of persons born before the mid-1930s, and for some born more recently, is the most perplexing dimension of the decision-making process in contemporary American society. This is the escalation of the rhetoric of communication to the degree that much of what is said is confusing rather than enlightening. The resulting credibility gap appears to be one of the most important factors constituting the context for decision-making in the 1970s and 1980s.

The Neo-Fundamentalists

In one sense what has happened is the emergence of a new group who may be described as the neo-fundamentalists of this decade. These are the people who typically were born before the mid-1930s and who have been trained to take literally what they are told.

Their ranks include the widowed mother of four who, on

the advice of a stockbroker employed by the largest brokerage firm in the nation, invested $4,800 in Stirling Homex, only to see that firm go bankrupt several months later.[2]

The ranks of these neo-fundamentalists include both the thousands of mothers on public assistance and the hundreds of well-intentioned middle-class do-gooders who saw on the horizon a new era made possible by the day care centers to be developed under the federally sponsored Work Incentive Program (WIN). It was promised that a mother on welfare would be able to leave her children at one of these centers and go out into the job market to earn enough money to improve her standard of living, and, hopefully, enough to enable her to leave the welfare rolls. The actual result was that many a welfare mother went out to a job paying less than $2 a hour to earn enough money to pay the salaries of middle-class teachers, social workers, and psychologists who received $5 to $10 an hour for taking care of her children.[3]

The ranks of these neo-fundamentalists also include the thousands of middle-class white churchmen who took literally the words in the famous Black Manifesto delivered by James Foreman. Their ranks include the millions who took literally the promises of three Presidents of the United States about the conflict in Southeast Asia. Their ranks include the thousands of grandfathers and grandmothers who gave generously out of their savings toward the construction costs of a new educational wing on their church because it was needed to relieve the overcrowding in the Sunday School, and then saw empty rooms Sunday after Sunday only a few years after completion of the new building.

The ranks of these neo-fundamentalists include those who believed in 1968 that business could solve the problem of providing decent housing for low-income families and at the same time bring blacks into the construction industry in much larger numbers, only to discover four years later that this was really nothing more than a new method for a large corporation, such as Boise Cascade, to lose nearly $40 million.

The ranks of these neo-fundamentalists include the young couple who eagerly transferred their membership to a new congregation in 1962 with the expectation that it would be free of the "hang-ups" and conservatism of their ninety-year-old downtown church, which seemed to be more concerned with institutional maintenance than with mission, only to discover twelve years later that the operational goals of this new congregation which now averages 128 at worship on Sunday morning are (1) to meet the monthly payments on the mortgage, (2) to raise enough money to maintain a full-time pastor, and (3) to pave the parking lot so it can also be used as an outdoor basketball court. Their ranks also include the millions of parents who chose their place of residence on the widely shared premise that the higher the per pupil expenditures of the school system, the better the quality of the education, only to be told later that the home is a far more important factor than the school in the educational achievements of children.

The ranks of these neo-fundamentalists include the people who worked eagerly to secure passage of a $4 million bond issue for construction of a new freeway in order to reduce traffic congestion, only to find that four years after the completion of the freeway traffic congestion is worse than ever. Their ranks include many who supported the "Great Society" programs of the 1960s in the expectation that these efforts would relieve the plight of the poor, only to discover a few years later that most of the money ended up in the pockets of middle-class professionals and semi-professionals. Their ranks include the thousands of proponents of industrial developments for creating new jobs, only to discover that the process has increased the rate of visible unemployment.

The growing disillusionment of these neo-fundamentalists, and the resulting credibility gap, are among the most significant factors that must be reckoned with in any attempt to describe the context for decision-making in the years ahead. Three other factors, each one at least in part a product of the recent escalation of the rhetoric, are an automatic distrust of any identifiable elite that seeks to influence the decision-making process, a growing distrust of planning as a means of solving problems, and a new, strong swing toward centralism.

This new movement toward centralism is also in part a normal swing of the pendulum, in part a reaction to the parochialism and the discriminatory practices that go with decentralism, and in part a product of the new elitism. Among the new forces fueling this current swing toward centralism are the contemporary ecology movement, the proponents of zero population growth, the several "liberation" movements, and the proponents of a redistribution of income. Each group finds that centralism can facilitate fulfillment of its goals while decentralization tends to impede the process.

Points of Tension

In looking at the context for decision-making in the years ahead, it may be possible to identify several points of probable tension.

One point of tension described earlier which undoubtedly will continue to exist is between the neo-fundamentalists who tend to take literally oral and written communications and the growing number of people who use language as much to express their feelings as to communicate in the more restricted traditional terms. This point of tension is a part of what has often been described in overly simplistic terms as "the generation gap." [4]

A second point of tension is between those who favor centralization and those who seek more decentralization; between those who favor the traditional style of "summit" or "top down" planning and those who favor a participatory or "bottom up" style of planning; [5] between those who support in practice what Michael Novak has described as rational authoritarianism[6] and those who favor a stronger voice for the popular will; and between the elitists and those who distrust the self-identified elites.[7] This point of tension was visible in the round of tinkering with the machinery described in chapter 4. It will be far more visible in the next round of re-structuring efforts.

A third point of tension in the decision-making process is, and will continue to be for years to come, between those who are primarily concerned with improving the quality or level of performance of the existing institutions and those who are primarily concerned with changing these existing institutions. This point of tension had remarkably high visibility in the 1964–72 period. (In the churches those concerned with change often identified themselves as proponents of "church renewal"; their political counterparts were identified as proponents of the "new politics.") In the 1970s, however, as more of those seriously concerned with planned change decide to work from "within the system," the tensions will be more severe, but less visible. One point of tension will be on interpretation of the agenda. One group will deal with the agenda from the perspective of performance, while the other will focus on change. A frequent result will be inadequate communication, since the messages will be sent back and forth on different wavelengths.

A fourth point of tension will be over the appropriate form of the planning that is to be a part of the total decision-making process. (The *form* of planning is to be distinguished from the *style* of planning. The conflicts over the style of planning, regardless of form, will emerge at the first point of tension described earlier.)

The traditional emphasis in planning has been on the allocation of scarce resources; one of the extreme examples of this form of planning in the churches was the allocation among several denominations of sites for new church development in the late 1950s and early 1960s. A better contemporary example of allocative planning in the churches is the use of such systems as planning-programming-budgeting or planning-budgeting-evaluation. Recent national discussions on planning for the use of energy resources, and the idea that a couple should have no more than two children, are other examples of allocative planning. The combination of hierarchical or elitist decision-making system and limited resources almost invariably means that (*a*) the form of the planning will be allocative and (*b*) there will be both "winners" and "losers" and the losers will be unhappy.

The emerging form of planning that is gaining an increasing number of adherents can be described as innovative planning.[8] Innovative planning is based on the assumption that planning should not be defined as "rational decision-making" as was the custom in the 1950s,[9] but rather as an approach to planned social change.[10]

A fifth point of tension that overlaps the first four on many occasions is between those who are making decisions which they hope will perpetuate or recapture yesterday and those who come to the decision-making table with a much stronger future orientation. In many congregations this is the point of tension that is already the most severe of any mentioned here.

Finally, the most baffling tensions will arise between the puzzling failures of some who practice a "rational authoritarianism" style of leadership and the successes of one group of leaders who use a benevolent autocratic style and another group who are very creative in opening up opportunities for meaningful participation by the "consumers" of decisions.[11] The real difference, however, and the distinction between success and failure, will probably not be related as much to differences in leadership styles as to distinctions between the one group of leaders who "push their product" and the other two groups of leaders who, despite radically different leadership styles, have a gift for identifying and responding to the needs of different groups of people. Style is often less important than substance when the evaluation is based on results!

In conclusion, two final comments should be made about the context for decision-making in the years ahead.

First, it will be vastly more complex than what is described in this chapter. People will not line up consistently on the same sides at every tension-producing point identified here. Furthermore, these divisions are not consistent within the dimension of time. At any given point in history some people at the decision-making table will be defending one side of one tension-producing division, while at the same time at the same table others will be speaking to one side of a completely different issue. One person may be advocating an innovative *form* of planning, while the person who is listening and developing a response is focusing his thoughts on a participatory *style* of planning. Another person at that table may be devoting all his thoughts to perpetuating the traditional allocations of resources.

Second, the participant who comes to the decision-making table with a carefully worked-out frame of reference for analyzing the decision-making process probably will have a clearer understanding of what is happening at that table, may be a more effective participant, and certainly should have more fun!

Notes

CHAPTER 1: HOW DECISIONS ARE MADE

1. Robert C. Weisselberg and Joseph G. Cowley, *The Executive Strategist* (New York: McGraw-Hill Book Co., 1969), pp. 39-51.
2. One insider contends that most of the decisions reaching a President of the United States are decisions, using this frame of reference, made under either conflict or uncertainty. See Theodore C. Sorensen, *Decision-Making in the White House* (New York: Columbia University Press, 1963), p. 11.
3. Talcott Parsons, *Structure and Process in Modern Societies* (New York: The Free Press of Glencoe, 1960), pp. 29-35.
4. Some readers may argue that the three centers should be labeled the congregation, the denomination, and international agencies. Most interdenominational agencies, however, resemble the United Nations, in that the visibility greatly exceeds the reality in impact.
5. For a more detailed examination of the steps in the process of planned change see Lyle E. Schaller, *The Change Agent* (Nashville: Abingdon Press, 1972), pp. 33-120.

CHAPTER 2: WHAT IS YOUR FRAME OF REFERENCE?

1. Quoted in an essay, "Another Professor with Power," *Time*, February 26, 1973, p. 80.
2. Page Smith, *The Historian and History* (New York: Alfred A. Knopf, 1964), p. 112.
3. Douglas W. Johnson and George W. Cornell, *Punctured Preconceptions* (New York, Friendship Press, 1972), p. 16.
4. *Ibid.*, pp. 68-71.
5. In a study of the attitudes of ministers and lay persons in central and southern Illinois a researcher asked individuals to respond to the statement "The Minister should carry out his regular pastoral calling in such a manner that members of his church regard his visits as just 'friendly personal chats.'" Slightly over 70 percent of the lay respondents and less than 20 percent of the ministers expressed agreement with that statement. S. Burkett Milner, "An Empirical Examination into the Ministerial Role Expectations of Clergy and Laity in the United Methodist Church of the Illinois Area," unpublished Ph.D. dissertation, Northwestern University, 1970.
6. For a more detailed discussion of this basic point see Andrew Hacker, "On Original Sin and Conservatives," *New York Times Magazine*, February 25, 1973.
7. A good beginning point on the debate over equality is the volume written by Christopher Jencks et al., *Inequality* (New York: Basic Books, 1972). Jencks contends that excessive demands have been placed on the public schools to reduce inequality among adults. For a brief review of the background and an analysis of how this re-

search divided the liberals who wrote the book see Angela Stent, "Cambridge's Radical Think Tank," *Change*, April 1973, pp. 34-37 and Godfrey Hodgson, "Do Schools Make a Difference?" *Atlantic*, March 1973, pp. 35-46. For a range of other responses to the debate see "Letters from Readers," *Commentary*, February 1973, pp. 12-25; the series of essays in *Social Policy*, May/June 1972, pp. 2-56; Samuel Bowles and Herbert Gintis, "I.Q. in the U. S. Class Structure," *Social Policy*, November/December 1972, January/February 1973, pp. 65-96; Frances Fox Piven and Richard A. Cloward, *Regulating the Poor: The Functions of Public Welfare* (New York: Pantheon Books, 1971); R. J. Herrnstein, "On Challenging an Orthodoxy," *Commentary*, April 1973, pp. 52-62; Maurice R. Berube and Marilyn Gittell, "In Whose Interest Is the Public Interest?" *Social Policy*, May/June 1970, pp. 5-9; David J. Armor, Thomas F. Pettigrew, and James Q. Wilson, "On Busing: An Exchange," *Public Interest*, Winter 1973, pp. 88-134; R. J. Herrnstein, *I. Q. in the Meritocracy* (Boston: Little, Brown, 1973); and Norman Daniels, "The Smart White Man's Burden," *Harper's*, October 1973, pp. 24-40.

8. "Walter Lippmann: An Interview with Ronald Steel," *New Republic*, April 14, 1973, pp. 16-21.

9. For a review of the Western idea of progress and social development see Robert A. Nisbet, *Social Change and History* (New York: Oxford University Press, 1969). For a succinct response to the excessively optimistic view of man that is inherent in liberalism, and to the excessively pessimistic view of man's rational capacity for justice that may lead to fascism, see Reinhold Niebuhr, *The Children of Light and the Children of Darkness* (New York: Charles Scribner's Sons, 1960).

10. For a more detailed discussion of this process see the chapter "Who's in Charge Here?" in Lyle E. Schaller, *The Pastor and the People* (Nashville: Abingdon Press, 1973), pp. 109-16.

11. For a more extended discussion of churches by types see Lyle E. Schaller, *Parish Planning* (Nashville: Abingdon Press, 1971), pp. 162-209.

CHAPTER 3: THE PRESSURES OF INSTITUTIONALISM

1. Quoted from J. Russell Hale, "The Making and Testing of an Organizational Saga: A Case Study of the Lutheran Theological Seminary at Gettysburg, Pennsylvania, with Special Reference to the Problem of Merger, 1959-1969," unpublished doctoral dissertation, Columbia University, 1970.

2. For an insight-filled account of the nature of institutional blight in the churches, universities, and foundations see Clarence H. Faust, "The Care and Feeding of Institutions," *Saturday Review*, March 30, 1968, pp. 12-16.

3. For an excellent analysis of goal subversion by institutional pressures in new churches see Donald L. Metz, *New Congregations* (Philadelphia: The Westminster Press, 1967).

4. For a classic study of how an idea for "doing good" can become institutionalized, commercialized, and a hazard to the people to be helped see the analysis of the procuring and distribution of blood in

Richard M. Titmuss, *The Gift Relationship* (New York: Pantheon Books, 1971).

5. James M. Wall, "A General Conference Report," *Behold*, October 1964, pp. 2-5.
6. For an extended discussion of this very basic point see Lon L. Fuller, "Two Principles of Human Associations," J. Roland Pennock and John W. Chapman, eds., *Voluntary Associations* (New York: Atherton Press, 1969), pp. 3-23.
7. H. Richard Niebuhr, *The Social Sources of Denominationalism* (New Gloucester, Mass.: Peter Smith, 1963).
8. Robert Lee, *The Social Sources of Church Unity* (Nashville: Abingdon Press, 1960).
9. For an evaluation by pastors of several of these functions see Douglas Johnson, "The Denomination: What's in It for Us?" *Christian Ministry*, May 1973, pp. 11-13.
10. Murray H. Leiffer, *The District Superintendent in The United Methodist Church* (Evanston: Bureau of Social and Religious Research, 1971), pp. 187-88.
11. Paul M. Harrison, *Authority and Power in the Free Church Tradition* (Carbondale, Ill.: Southern Illinois University Press, 1971).
12. For an excellent brief introduction to organizational patterns in the major religious faiths in America see Gibson Winter, *Religious Identity* (New York: The Macmillan Co., 1968).

CHAPTER 4: TINKERING WITH THE MACHINERY

1. For an appraisal of the Charismatic Renewal Movement see Lyle E. Schaller, "Will the Third Great Awakening Miss the Churches?" *Together*, May 1973, pp. 15-16.
2. Decision number 364 of the Judicial Council of The United Methodist Church.
3. Decision number 359 of the Judicial Council of The United Methodist Church.
4. The emotional turmoil experienced by veteran church bureaucrats is revealed very clearly in a perceptive essay by Denis E. Shoemaker, "Ecclesiastical Future Shock: The Ordeal of Restructuring." *Christian Century*, March 14, 1973, pp. 312-15.
5. Decision number 356 of the Jucicial Council of The United Methodist Church.
6. For an analysis of the pros and cons of quotas as used by one denomination see Charles A. Sayre, "United Methodism's Quotas: They Should Be Temporary," *Christian Advocate*, April 12, 1973, pp. 7-8.
7. For an interesting debate on the issue of large versus small conventions and related issues see Frederick K. Wentz, "Small Conventions a Serious Mistake," and Frank K. Zimmerman, "Large Conventions Are Ineffective," *Lutheran*, March 7, 1973, pp. 20-24.
8. For a brief statement on behalf of the values of an optimal degree of redundancy in a complex system see Lyle E. Schaller, *Parish Planning* (Nashville: Abingdon Press, 1971), pp. 221-40.
9. The reader who may be interested in pursuing the philosophical basis

for this section may find it helpful to read, perhaps in this sequence, Gordon Tullock, *The Politics of Bureaucracy* (Washington: Public Affairs Press, 1965); Anthony Downs, *Inside Bureaucracy* (Boston: Little Brown, 1967); Peter B. Clark and James Q. Wilson, "Incentive Systems: A Theory of Organization," *Administrative Science Quarterly*, September 1961, pp. 154-61; C. Northcote Parkinson, *Parkinson's Law and Other Studies in Administration* (Boston: Houghton Mifflin, 1957; and William A. Niskanen, Jr. ed., *Bureaucracy and Representative Government* (Chicago: Aldine-Atherton, 1971).

CHAPTER 5: POLITY, POLITICS, AND PATRONAGE

1. This is not a completely original observation by any means! For example, a report by the Ad Interim Committee on Institutional Forms (January 1966) of the Presbyterian Church in the U.S. contained the statement "The fact is that many of our people are at heart congregationalists." *New Wineskins*, p. 11.

2. Paul M. Harrison, *Authority and Power in the Free Church Tradition* (Carbondale, Ill.: Southern Illinois University Press, 1971). This book offers a carefully researched study of the discrepancy between the tradition and form which suggest a strong congregational type of polity and the substance which resembles the social structure of big business or big government.

3. In examining this issue one scholar concluded there is no such thing as *the* New Testament form of church order. See Edward Schweizer, *Church Order in the New Testament* (Naperville, Ill.: Alec R. Allenson, 1961).

4. Peter H. Rossi and Robert A. Dentler, *The Politics of Urban Renewal* (New York: The Free Press of Glencoe, 1961), p. 7. For the classic definition of politics see Harold D. Lasswell, *Politics: Who Gets What, When, How* (New York: World Publishing Co., 1958).

5. John D. B. Miller, *The Nature of Politics* (Chicago: Encyclopaedia Brittanica Press, 1964), p. 14. For another useful definition of politics that can be adapted very easily to the decision-making process in the churches see Michael Walzer, *Obligations* (Cambridge: Harvard University Press, 1970), p. 201.

6. Keith R. Bridston, *Church Politics* (New York: World Publishing Co., 1969), p. 10.

7. *Ibid.*, pp. 140-64.

8. For a historically based definition of patronage see William Safire, *The New Language of Politics* (New York: Random House, 1968), pp. 323-24.

9. For a more detailed explanation of the crucial political importance of the deference pyramid see Lasswell, *Politics*, pp. 13-27.

10. Joseph Mitchell, "The Story of the 1948 Elections to the Episcopacy," *Christian Advocate*, February 3, 1972, p. 14.

11. Some of the background for this change in *The Discipline* of The Methodist Church can be found in a study which revealed that several Methodist bishops were keenly aware of the feeling among some delegates to the jurisdictional conferences that "if we can elect our man, he'll take care of his friends." This feeling was sufficiently strong that many bishops supported the proposal that a newly elected

bishop should not be assigned to the area where he had served before election. Murray H. Leiffer, "The Episcopacy in the Present
Day," *The Study of the General Superintendency of The Methodist
Church* (Evanston, Ill.: Bureau of Social and Religious Research,
1963), pp. 31-33.
12. Mitchell, "1948 Elections," pp. 12-14.
13. For a critical evaluation of the Roman ballot by the former president
of The American Lutheran Church see the essay by Frederick A.
Schiotz, *Commentator*, August 1966, p. 4.

CHAPTER 6: INTERCHURCH COOPERATION

1. A statement opposing tax credits was filed by a staff person of the
National Council in April, 1973. Most of it was drawn from an official
1961 NCC position paper. A month later the statement was repudiated
by the general secretary of the National Council, following a protest by
a Catholic bishop.
   For a scholarly analysis of the National Council of Churches see
Henry J. Pratt, *The Liberalization of American Protestantism* (Detroit:
Wayne State University Press, 1972).
2. James D. Glasse, *Putting It Together in the Parish* (Nashville: Abingdon Press, 1972), pp. 55-61.

CHAPTER 7: DOLLARS AND DECISIONS

1. Quoted in Roger Ricklefs, "Emphasis on Efficiency at Time, Inc. Has
Many Shaking in Their Boots" *Wall Street Journal*, February 12, 1973.
2. For an elaboration on the value and role of the interim pastor see
Lyle E. Schaller, *The Pastor and the People* (Nashville: Abingdon Press,
1973), pp. 56-64.
3. For a very revealing and helpful essay on this switch from increasing
receipts to cutting costs see Ernest Holsendolph, "A Tale of Two Universities," *Fortune*, February 1971. In this essay the contrast is drawn
between the tradition of responding to increases in expenses at Yale
by increasing income and at the University of Southern California by
cutting costs. The author goes on to point out that in recent years
Yale has had to give far more attention to cutting costs than had
been the tradition.
4. PPB was terminated in the federal government by a circular from the
Office of Management and Budget (OMB) as part of an effort to
simplify the budget submission requirements. For a review of the
merits and the shortcomings of PPB and an analysis of why federal
agencies have moved away from it see Allen Schick, "A Death in the
Bureaucracy: The Demise of Federal PPB," *Public Administration Review*, March/April 1973, pp. 146-56.
5. For an analysis of how denominational judicatories began to use the
budget as a place for resolving conflict see Lyle E. Schaller, "The
New Style Attack on the Denominational Budget," *Christian Century*,
November 26, 1969, pp. 1515-18.
6. For another approach used by some congregations to tie together the
setting of program priorities and underwriting the total financial pro-

gram of the congregation see Schaller, *The Pastor and the People*, pp. 166-67.

7. For a provocative analysis of the limitations of bureaucracies see William A. Niskanen, Jr., ed., *Bureaucracy and Representative Government* (Chicago: Aldine-Atherton, 1971). For another statement on "contracting out" for services see Peter Drucker, "Can the Businessman Meet Our Social Needs?" *Saturday Review of the Society*, April 1973, pp. 43-44.

CHAPTER 8: FRIENDS, PASTORS, LEADERS, AND MANAGERS

1. One indication of the harm that may have been done is described in Morton Lieberman, Irvin Yalom, and Matthew Miles, *Encounter Groups: First Facts* (New York: Basic Books, 1973).

2. Elton Mayo, *The Human Problems of an Industrial Civilization* (New York: Viking Press, 1960).

3. Kurt Lewin, *Field Theory in Social Science* (New York: Harper & Row, 1951); Kurt Lewin, *Resolving Social Conflicts*, ed. Gertrud Weiss Lewin and Gordon W. Allport (New York: Harper & Row, 1948).

4. Douglas McGregor, *The Human Side of Enterprise* (New York: McGraw-Hill Book Co., 1960). For a sympathetic but critical evaluation of McGregor's contributions see Warren G. Bennis, "Chairman Mac in Perspective," *Harvard Business Review*, September/October 1972, pp. 140-49.

5. Elliott Jaques, *Work, Creativity and Social Justice* (New York: International Universities Press, 1970) and Harry Levinson, *The Exceptional Executive* (Cambridge: Harvard University Press, 1968).

6. Two excellent books on organizational development growing out of two different perspectives are Harvey A. Hornstein, et al., *Social Intervention* (New York: The Free Press, 1971) and Harry Levinson, *Organizational Diagnosis* (Cambridge: Harvard University Press, 1972). The first is written from a behavioral science approach, and the second is derived from psychoanalytic theory.

7. For an example of how the application of encounter-group methodology failed to change a religious institution see William R. Coulson, *Groups, Gimmicks and Instant Gurus* (New York: Harper & Row, 1972), pp. 99-142.

8. I am indebted to Dick Lavender for this diagram.

9. Frederick Herzberg et al., *The Motivation to Work* (New York: John Wiley & Sons, 1959).

10. For an interesting discussion of the contemporary Machiavellis see Richard Christie, "The Machiavellis Among Us," *Psychology Today*, November 1970, p. 82. For an attempt to suggest how contemporary organizations parallel the medieval dukedoms in behavior patterns see Antony Jay, *Management and Machiavelli: An Inquiry into the Politics of Corporate Life* (New York: Holt, Rinehart and Winston, 1968).

11. B. F. Skinner, *Beyond Freedom and Dignity* (New York: Alfred A. Knopf, 1971).

12. Harry Levinson, *The Great Jackass Fallacy* (Boston: Graduate School of Business Administration, Harvard University, 1973), pp. 10-11.

13. Gerald J. Jud, "The Local Church and the Big Daddy Fantasy,"

Crisis in the Church, ed. Everett C. Parker (Philadelphia: Pilgrim Press, 1968), pp. 39-49. For a more recent analysis of Big Daddy's death see Lyle E. Schaller, *The Change Agent* (Nashville: Abingdon Press, 1972), pp. 126-28.

14. Quoted in Warren Bennis, *Organization Development: Its Nature, Origins and Prospects* (Reading, Mass.: Addison-Wesley Publishing Co., 1969), p. 76.

15. Miriam Rodin and Burton Rodin, "Student Evaluation of Teachers," *Science*, September 29, 1972, pp. 1164-66.

16. George S. Odiorne, *Management Decisions by Objectives* (Englewood Cliffs, N.J.: Prentice-Hall, 1969), pp. 102-5.

17. For an outstanding discussion of the criteria for delegating authority see Robert A. Dahl, *After the Revolution?* (New Haven: Yale University Press, 1970).

18. For an elaboration of this point see Schaller, *The Pastor and the People*, pp. 80-86.

19. For an excellent analysis of the several roles of the pastor see Seward Hiltner, *Ferment in the Ministry* (Nashville: Abingdon Press, 1969).

20. Sorensen, *Decision-Making in the White House*, pp. 22-23.

21. Thomas Shepphard, "Working Your Way Up Through the Groan, the Wolf Pack, and the Dog and the Lamp Post," *Management Review*, November 1972, pp. 30-42.

22. For a brief summary of one body of research which suggests that leadership training has not been very effective see Fred E. Fiedler, "The Trouble with Leadership Training Is It Doesn't Train Leaders," *Psychology Today*, February 1973, pp. 29 ff.

23. Robert Heller, *The Great Executive Dream: The First Myth of Management Is That It Exists* (New York: Delacorte Press, 1972). Among Heller's ten points is "No executive devotes effort to proving himself wrong." Martin R. Smith, *I Hate to See a Manager Cry: or, How to Prevent the Litany of Management from Fouling Up Your Career* (Reading, Mass.: Addison-Wesley Publishing Co., 1973). Among the several useful tools relevant to the churches described by Smith in clear and succinct terminology are Short-Interval Scheduling and the distinction between effectiveness and efficiency. For an optimistic and pluralistic analysis of the effective leader see Harlan Cleveland, *The Future Executive* (New York: Harper & Row, 1972). Cleveland stresses ambiguity as the context for management and describes the ideal manager for a tomorrow filled with ambiguity as one who is "collegial, consensual and consultative" in his style.

24. Both quotations are from Philip B. Crosby, *The Art of Getting Your Own Sweet Way* (New York: McGraw-Hill Book Co., 1972).

25. Levinson, *The Great Jackass Fallacy*, p. 29.

26. For an excellent brief and critical analysis of McGregor's contributions to management see Warren G. Bennis, "Chairman Mac in Perspective," *Harvard Business Review*, September/October, 1972, pp. 140-49.

CHAPTER 9: EVALUATION AND ACCOUNTABILITY

1. A 1965 Gallup Poll of religious attitudes and behavior patterns replicated a 1952 survey, and one of the questions asked was whether the respon-

dent had always been a member of the same denomination or had changed denominations. In 1952, 79 percent said they had always been a member of the same denomination and had not changed. In 1965 this figure was 80 percent. Half of those reporting that they had changed denominations said it was because of either changing to the spouse's church or moving to a community where their denomination did not have a church or another church was more conveniently located. In 1952, 82 percent of the Baptist respondents said they had always been Baptists, compared to 85 percent in 1965. In 1952, 78 percent of the Methodist respondents said they had always been Methodists, compared to 80 percent in 1965. In 1952, 80 percent of the Lutheran respondents said they had always been Lutherans, compared to 75 percent thirteen years later. In 1952, 73 percent of the Presbyterian respondents said they had always been Presbyterians, compared to 66 percent thirteen years later. Martin E. Marty et al, *What Do We Believe?* (New York: Meredith Press, 1968), pp, 304-6. In general, the larger the denomination the larger the percentage of members who have not changed their denominational affiliation. In the smaller denominations only 60 to 70 percent of the members have not changed denominational affiliation sometime during their lifetime. The probable reason is that a larger percentage change because of marriage or because they moved to a community in which there is no church of their denomination.

2. Alice M. Rivlin, *Systematic Thinking for Social Action* (Washington: The Brookings Institution, 1971), pp. 120-44.
3. Much of this "new realism" was evoked by the failures of some of the grand designs of the Great Society programs of the Lyndon B. Johnson era. For an insider's analysis see Robert A. Levine, "Rethinking Our Social Strategies," *Public Interest*, Winter 1968, pp. 88-92. For an argument in favor of localism see Milton Kotler, *Neighborhood Government* (Indianapolis: Bobbs-Merrill, 1969).
4. For a series of questions that may be used in evaluating the structures and the accountability systems of denominational and interdenominational agencies see Lyle E. Schaller, "Organizing for Mission," in *Toward Creative Urban Strategy*, ed. George A. Torney (Waco, Tex. Word Books, 1970), pp. 214-32.
5. For another frame of reference for evaluation see S. Prakash Sethi, "Getting a Handle on the Social Audit," *Business and Society Review/Innovation*, Winter 1972-73, pp. 31-38. For guidelines on a congregational evaluation see Lyle E. Schaller, "Principles in Congregational Self-Evaluation," *Christian Ministry*, January 1973, pp. 20-23.

CHAPTER 10: THE CONTEXT FOR TOMORROW

1. *Attica: The Official Report of the New York State Special Commission on Attica* (New York: Bantam Books, 1972).
2. Michael J. Connor, "Wall Street Analysts Give Lots of Bad Advice Along with the Good," *Wall Street Journal*, May 25, 1973, pp. 1, 22.
3. Sheila M. Rothman, "Other People's Children: The Day Care Experience in America," *Public Interest*, Winter 1973, pp. 11-40.
4. For a view that relates the generation gap to a point in history rather than to youth see Margaret Mead, "The Oldest Postwar People," *New York Times*, January 21, 1973.

5. The best single item on the evolution of planning styles is John Friedman, *Retracking America: A Theory of Transactive Planning* (Garden City: Anchor Press/Doubleday, 1973), pp. 1-21, 49-84.

6. Michael Novak, *The Rise of the Unmeltable Ethnics* (New York: The Macmillan Co., 1973), p. 259.

7. For an excellent review of the general shift from the pluralism of the 1950s to the greater acceptance by political scientists of a hierarchical distribution of power and of power elites see Kenneth Prewitt and Alan Stone, *The Ruling Elites* (New York: Harper & Row, 1973). Prewitt and Stone are less critical of contemporary elites than are Friedmann and Novak.

8. The terms to describe these forms of planning are borrowed from Friedmann, *Retracking America*, pp. 49-70.

9. For a couple of influential examples of the traditional definitions of planning see Rexford G. Tugwell and Edward C. Banfield, "Governmental Planning at Mid-Century," *Journal of Politics*, vol. 13, 1951, pp. 133-63, and Herbert A. Simon, *Administrative Behavior* (New York: The Free Press, 1957), pp. 99-102, 228-34. The serious student of decision-making in complex organizations will find Simon's book somewhat dated, but very provocative in helping the reader improve his own frame of reference.

10. For an introduction to the concept of the leader as an agent of intentional change see Lyle E. Schaller, *The Change Agent* (Nashville: Abingdon Press, 1972).

11. For an imaginative and extremely well organized analysis of creative innovation see Theodore Levitt, *The Marketing Mode* (New York: McGraw-Hill Book Co., 1969), especially pp. 158-59 and 185-86.

Index